THE PENGUIN
EDITED FROM THE
BY G. B. HA
B23
LOVE'S LABOUR'S LOST

2052

WILLIAM SHAKESPEARE

Love's Labour's Lost

PENGUIN BOOKS

Penguin Books Ltd, Harmondsworth, Middlesex, England
Penguin Books Australia Ltd, Ringwood, Victoria, Australia

—

This edition first published 1953
Reprinted, 1969

—

Made and printed in Great Britain
by Cox & Wyman Ltd,
London, Fakenham and Reading

The Editor gratefully acknowledges
the kindness of Dr J. C. Adams in
allowing the Penguin Shakespeare to
reproduce an engraving of his
model of the stage of the
Globe Playhouse

The portraits on th e cover and on the title page
were engraved by Reynolds Stone

—

This book is sold subject to the condition
that it shall not, by way of trade or otherwise,
be lent, re-sold, hired out, or otherwise circulated
without the publisher's prior consent in any form of
binding or cover other than that in which it is
published and without a similar condition
including this condition being imposed
on the subsequent purchaser

CONTENTS

★

THE WORKS OF SHAKESPEARE

APPROXIMATE DATE	PLAYS		FIRST PRINTED
Before 1594	HENRY VI *three parts*		*Folio* 1623
	RICHARD III		1597
	TITUS ANDRONICUS		1594
	LOVE'S LABOUR'S LOST		1598
	THE TWO GENTLEMEN OF VERONA		*Folio*
	THE COMEDY OF ERRORS		*Folio*
	THE TAMING OF THE SHREW		*Folio*
1594–1597	ROMEO AND JULIET	(*pirated* 1597)	1599
	A MIDSUMMER NIGHT'S DREAM		1600
	RICHARD II		1597
	KING JOHN		*Folio*
	THE MERCHANT OF VENICE		1600
1597–1600	HENRY IV *part i*		1598
	HENRY IV *part ii*		1600
	HENRY V	(*pirated* 1600)	*Folio*
	MUCH ADO ABOUT NOTHING		1600
	MERRY WIVES OF WINDSOR	(*pirated* 1602)	*Folio*
	AS YOU LIKE IT		*Folio*
	JULIUS CAESAR		*Folio*
	TROYLUS AND CRESSIDA		1609
1601–1608	HAMLET	(*pirated* 1603)	1604
	TWELFTH NIGHT		*Folio*
	MEASURE FOR MEASURE		*Folio*
	ALL'S WELL THAT ENDS WELL		*Folio*
	OTHELLO		1622
	LEAR		1608
	MACBETH		*Folio*
	TIMON OF ATHENS		*Folio*
	ANTONY AND CLEOPATRA		*Folio*
	CORIOLANUS		*Folio*
After 1608	PERICLES	(*omitted from the Folio*)	1609
	CYMBELINE		*Folio*
	THE WINTER'S TALE		*Folio*
	THE TEMPEST		*Folio*
	HENRY VIII		*Folio*

POEMS

DATES UNKNOWN	VENUS AND ADONIS	1593
	THE RAPE OF LUCRECE	1594
	SONNETS A LOVER'S COMPLAINT	1609
	THE PHOENIX AND THE TURTLE	1601

WILLIAM SHAKESPEARE

William Shakespeare was born at Stratford upon Avon in April, 1564. He was the third child, and eldest son, of John Shakespeare and Mary Arden. His father was one of the most prosperous men of Stratford, who held in turn the chief offices in the town. His mother was of gentle birth, the daughter of Robert Arden of Wilmcote. In December, 1582, Shakespeare married Ann Hathaway, daughter of a farmer of Shottery, near Stratford; their first child Susanna was baptized on May 6, 1583, and twins, Hamnet and Judith, on February 22, 1585. Little is known of Shakespeare's early life; but it is unlikely that a writer who dramatized such an incomparable range and variety of human kinds and experiences should have spent his early manhood entirely in placid pursuits in a country town. There is one tradition, not universally accepted, that he fled from Stratford because he was in trouble for deer stealing, and had fallen foul of Sir Thomas Lucy, the local magnate; another that he was for some time a schoolmaster.

From 1592 onwards the records are much fuller. In March, 1592, the Lord Strange's players produced a new play at the Rose Theatre called *Harry the Sixth*, which was very successful, and was probably the *First Part of Henry VI*. In the autumn of 1592 Robert Greene, the best known of the professional writers, as he was dying wrote a letter to three fellow writers in which he warned them against the ingratitude of players in general, and in particular against an 'upstart crow' who 'supposes he is as much able to bombast out a blank verse as the best of you: and being an absolute Johannes Factotum is in his own conceit the only Shake-scene in a country.' This is the first reference to Shakespeare, and the whole passage suggests that Shakespeare had become suddenly famous as a playwright. At this time Shakespeare was brought into touch with Edward Alleyne the great tragedian, and Christopher Marlowe, whose thundering parts of Tamburlaine, the Jew of Malta and Dr Faustus Alleyne was acting, as well as Hieronimo, the hero of Kyd's *Spanish Tragedy*, the most famous of all Elizabethan plays.

In April, 1593, Shakespeare published his poem *Venus and Adonis*, which was dedicated to the young Earl of Southampton: it was a great and lasting success, and was reprinted nine times in the next few years. In May, 1594, his second poem, *The Rape of Lucrece*, was also dedicated to Southampton.

There was little playing in 1593, for the theatres were shut during a severe outbreak of the plague; but in the autumn of 1594, when the plague ceased, the playing companies were reorganized, and Shakespeare became a sharer in the Lord Chamberlain's company who went to play in the Theatre in Shoreditch. During these months Marlowe and Kyd had died. Shakespeare was thus for a time without a rival. He had already written the three parts of *Henry VI, Richard III, Titus Andronicus, The Two Gentlemen of Verona, Love's Labour's Lost, The Comedy of Errors*, and *The Taming of the Shrew*. Soon afterwards he wrote the first of his greater plays – *Romeo and Juliet* – and he followed this success in the next three years with *A Midsummer Night's Dream, Richard II*, and *The Merchant of Venice*. The two parts of *Henry VI*, introducing Falstaff, the most popular of all his comic characters, were written in 1597–8.

The company left the Theatre in 1597 owing to disputes

over a renewal of the ground lease, and went to play at the Curtain in the same neighbourhood. The disputes continued throughout 1598, and at Christmas the players settled the matter by demolishing the old Theatre and re-erecting a new playhouse on the South bank of the Thames, near Southwark Cathedral. This playhouse was named the Globe. The expenses of the new building were shared by the chief members of the Company, including Shakespeare, who was now a man of some means. In 1596 he had bought New Place, a large house in the centre of Stratford, for £60, and through his father purchased a coat-of-arms from the Heralds, which was the official recognition that he and his family were gentlefolk.

By the summer of 1598 Shakespeare was recognized as the greatest of English dramatists. Booksellers were printing his more popular plays, at times even in pirated or stolen versions, and he received a remarkable tribute from a young writer named Francis Meres, in his book *Palladis Tamia*. In a long catalogue of English authors Meres gave Shakespeare more prominence than any other writer, and mentioned by name twelve of his plays.

Shortly before the Globe was opened, Shakespeare had completed the cycle of plays dealing with the whole story of the Wars of the Roses with *Henry V*. It was followed by *As You Like it,* and *Julius Caesar,* the first of the maturer tragedies. In the next three years he wrote *Troilus and Cressida, The Merry Wives of Windsor, Hamlet,* and *Twelfth Night.*

On March 24, 1603, Queen Elizabeth died. The company had often performed before her, but they found her successor a far more enthusiastic patron. One of the first acts of King James was to take over the company and to promote them to be his own servants so that henceforward they were known as the King's Men. They acted now very frequently at Court, and prospered accordingly. In the early years of the reign Shakespeare wrote the more sombre comedies, *All's Well that Ends Well,* and *Measure for Measure,* which were followed by *Othello, Macbeth,* and *King Lear.* Then he returned to Roman themes with *Antony and Cleopatra* and *Coriolanus.*

Since 1601 Shakespeare had been writing less, and there were now a number of rival dramatists who were introducing new styles of drama, particularly Ben Jonson (whose first successful comedy, *Every Man in his Humour,* was acted by Shakespeare's company in 1598), Chapman, Dekker, Marston, and Beaumont and Fletcher who began to write in 1607. In 1608 the King's Men acquired a second playhouse, an indoor private theatre in the fashionable quarter of the Blackfriars. At private theatres, plays were performed indoors; the prices charged were higher than in the public playhouses, and the audience consequently was more select. Shakespeare seems to have retired from the stage about this time: his name does not occur in the various lists of players after 1607. Henceforward he lived for the most part at Stratford, where he was regarded as one of the most important citizens. He still wrote a few plays, and he tried his hand at the new form of tragi-comedy – a play with tragic incidents but a happy ending – which Beaumont and Fletcher had popularized. He wrote four of these – *Pericles, Cymbeline, The Winter's Tale,* and *The Tempest,* which was acted at Court in 1611. For the last four years of his life he lived in retirement. His son Hamnet had died in 1596: his two daughters were now married. Shakespeare died at Stratford upon Avon on April 23, 1616, and was buried in the chancel of the church, before the high altar. Shortly afterwards a memorial which still exists, with a portrait bust, was set up on the North wall. His wife survived him.

When Shakespeare died fourteen of his plays had been separately published in Quarto booklets. In 1623 his surviving fellow actors, John Heming and Henry Condell, with the co-operation of a number of printers, published a collected edition of thirty-six plays in one Folio volume, with an engraved portrait, memorial verses by Ben Jonson and others, and an Epistle to the Reader in which Heming and Condell make the interesting note that Shakespeare's 'hand and mind went together, and what he thought, he uttered with that easiness that we have scarce received from him a blot in his papers.'

The plays as printed in the Quartos or the Folio differ considerably from the usual modern text. They are often not divided into scenes, and sometimes not even into acts. Nor are there place-headings at the beginning of each scene, because in the Elizabethan theatre there was no scenery. They are carelessly printed and the spelling is erratic.

THE ELIZABETHAN THEATRE

Although plays of one sort and another had been acted for many generations, no permanent playhouse was erected in England until 1576. In the 1570's the Lord Mayor and Aldermen of the City of London and the players were constantly at variance. As a result James Burbage, then the leader of the great Earl of Leicester's players, decided that he would erect a playhouse outside the jurisdiction of the Lord Mayor, where the players would no longer be hindered by the authorities. Accordingly in 1576 he built the Theatre in Shoreditch, at that time a suburb of London.

The experiment was successful, and by 1592 there were two more playhouses in London, the Curtain (also in Shoreditch), and the Rose on the south bank of the river, near Southwark Cathedral.

Elizabethan players were accustomed to act on a variety of stages; in the great hall of a nobleman's house, or one of the Queen's palaces, in town halls and in yards, as well as their own theatre.

The public playhouse for which most of Shakespeare's plays were written was a small and intimate affair. The outside measurement of the Fortune Theatre, which was built in 1600 to rival the new Globe, was but eighty feet square. Playhouses were usually circular or octagonal, with three tiers of galleries looking down upon the yard or pit, which was open to the sky. The stage jutted out into the yard so that the actors came forward into the midst of their audience.

Over the stage there was a roof, and on either side doors by which the characters entered or disappeared. Over the back of the stage ran a gallery or upper stage which was used whenever an upper scene was needed, as when Romeo climbs up to Juliet's bedroom, or the citizens of Angiers address King John from the walls. The space beneath this upper stage was known as the tiring house; it was concealed from the audience by a curtain which would be drawn back to reveal an inner stage, for such scenes as the witches' cave in Macbeth, Prospero's cell or Juliet's tomb.

There was no general curtain concealing the whole stage, so that all scenes on the main stage began with an entrance and ended with an exit. Thus in tragedies the dead must be carried away. There was no scenery, and therefore no limit to the number of scenes, for a scene came to an end when the characters left the stage. When it was necessary for the

THE GLOBE THEATRE

Wood-engraving by R. J. Beedham after a reconstruction by J. C. Adams

exact locality of a scene to be known, then Shakespeare indicated it in the dialogue; otherwise a simple property or a garment was sufficient; a chair or stool showed an indoor scene, a man wearing riding boots was a messenger, a king wearing armour was on the battlefield, or the like. Such simplicity was on the whole an advantage; the spectator was not distracted by the setting and Shakespeare was able to use as many scenes as he wished. The action passed by very quickly: a play of 2500 lines of verse could be acted in two hours. Moreover, since the actor was so close to his audience, the slightest subtlety of voice and gesture was easily appreciated.

The company was a 'Fellowship of Players', who were all partners and sharers. There were usually ten to fifteen full members, with three or four boys, and some paid servants. Shakespeare had therefore to write for his team. The chief actor in the company was Richard Burbage, who first distinguished himself as Richard III; for him Shakespeare wrote his great tragic parts. An important member of the company was the clown or low comedian. From 1594 to 1600 the company's clown was Will Kemp; he was succeeded by Robert Armin. No women were allowed to appear on the stage, and all women's parts were taken by boys.

*

LOVE'S LABOUR'S LOST

The earliest known edition of *Love's Labour's Lost* is a quarto, dated 1598, and entitled *A Pleasant Conceited Comedie Called, Loues labors lost. As it was presented before her Highness this last Christmas. Newly corrected and augmented By W. Shakespere. Imprinted at London by W. W. for Cutbert Burby. 1598*. There is no entry in the Stationers' Register and the words 'newly corrected and augmented' on the title-page imply that at least one earlier edition had appeared; but if so, no copy survives. A similar note occurs in the second quarto of *Romeo and Juliet* which differs considerably from the first. The second quarto of *I Henry IV* is also described as newly corrected although the corrections are only of misprints.

There are, however, internal evidences of revision in the play itself. In Berowne's speech to the perjured lovers (IV. 3), the passage (p. 72, l. 33) beginning 'And where that you have vowed . . .' to (p. 73, l. 21) 'our learning there' is duplicated in what follows ('we have made . . . proves excellent'). Similarly Berowne's few words to Rosaline and her reply (p. 108, l. 1) 'what to me . . . people sick' are greatly expanded a few lines later (p. 108, l. 22 – p. 109, l. 23) in the speeches beginning 'Studies my Lady... in an Hospital.'

The date of the play is doubtful. The title-page of the quarto establishes that it was written before Christmas 1597, but there is no unanimity among scholars who have guessed various dates from 1588 to 1596. The style of the play – if style in a play so out of the ordinary is any guide –

would link *Love's Labour's Lost* with the Sonnets and the earlier plays such as *Romeo and Juliet*. The many topicalities and the jokes obviously intended for a select audience suggest that the play was originally written for private performance at Court, or some Great House, or for the Inns of Court.

The play abounds with topicalities. Some seem obvious; most are inexplicable without a clue. The characters – though several of them are the stock figures of Italian comedy – are to some extent caricatures and would have suggested amusing parallels to the original audience. The four young men, for instance, are named Navarre, Berowne, Dumain, and Longaville. Many young Englishmen had served in the wars in France with the small expeditionary forces which were aiding Henri of Navarre in 1591 and 1592. Among the notable figures in the campaign were the Marshal de Biron and the Duc de Longueville, two of Navarre's chief commanders, and the Duc du Mayne, his most powerful opponent. It was an amusing notion in itself to bring this ill-assorted company together to study philosophy and to avoid the society of women, especially as the real Navarre was notorious for his love affairs, and constantly embarrassed by the demands of his various ladies.

Of the others, Armado has been variously identified with Sir Walter Raleigh, Don Antonio the ex-King of Portugal, and Antonio Perez, former Secretary to the King of Spain amongst others. Much would have originally depended on the make-up and mannerisms affected by the actor. Shakespeare, however, seldom indulged in continuous and consistent caricature; a word, a reminder, or a gesture to raise a laugh, and then the character steps back into his proper part.

A topicality which can reasonably be identified is to be found in IV. iii (p. 71, l. 20) in the lines:

> O paradox, Black is the badge of hell,
> The hue of dungeons, and the School of night.

In the 1590's much scandal was caused by a coterie of intellectuals, of whom Raleigh was chief, who were accused of discussing various obscure and forbidden topics. Other members of the group were Henry Percy, Earl of Northumberland, known as the Wizard Earl, a keen student of the sciences; Thomas Harriott, one of the greatest mathematicians of the age; and the two poets, Christopher Marlowe and George Chapman. The speculations of this group were much noted and suspected. It was said that, with Harriott as their schoolmaster, certain young gentlemen were taught to make a jest of the Scriptures, to ridicule such articles of faith as the immortality of the soul and the future life, and amongst other things to spell the name of God backwards. In 1594 Chapman published an obscure poem called *The Shadow of Night* which he dedicated to Matthew Roydon, another member of the group.

No source for the story of the play has been found and it is probable that Shakespeare invented it.

Of the two texts, the quarto has been claimed as a direct print from Shakespeare's own manuscript, but it contains many small errors. The Folio text is more carefully printed and shows some traces of revision after the publication of the quarto. In this text the Folio has been followed closely. It is, on the whole, well printed except that the compositor was not very successful with the Latin and Italian tags; these, following the usual practice, have been reproduced as set right by editors. Spelling has been conservatively modernized; but the original punctuation and arrangement have been kept except where they seemed manifestly wrong. A few phrases which the Folio has omitted are marked by [ ]. The reader will find some differences between this and the usual text, but the result is nearer to what Shakespeare wrote.

Love's Labour's Lost

THE ACTORS' NAMES

FERDINAND, King of Navarre

BEROWNE,
LONGAVILLE, } lords attending on the King
DUMAIN,

BOYET,
MARCADE, } lords attending on the Princess of France

OTHER LORDS

DON ADRIANO DE ARMADO, the Braggart

SIR NATHANIEL, the Curate

HOLOFERNES, the Pedant

DULL, the Constable

COSTARD, the Clown

MOTH, the Boy, page to Armado

A Forester

THE PRINCESS of France

ROSALINE,
MARIA, } ladies attending on the Princess
KATHARINE,

JAQUENETTA, a country wench

Enter Ferdinand, King of Navarre, Berowne, Longaville,
and Dumain.

KING: Let Fame, that all hunt after in their lives,
Live register'd upon our brazen tombs,
And then grace us in the disgrace of death:
When spite of cormorant devouring Time,
Th' endeavour of this present breath may buy
That honour which shall bate his scythe's keen edge,
And make us heirs of all eternity.
Therefore brave conquerors, for so you are,
That war against your own affections,
And the huge army of the world's desires,
Our late edict shall strongly stand in force,
Navarre shall be the wonder of the world.
Our Court shall be a little Academe,
Still and contemplative in living art.
You three, Berowne, Dumain, and Longaville,
Have sworn for three years' term, to live with me:
My fellow scholars, and to keep those statutes
That are recorded in this schedule here.
Your oaths are pass'd, and now subscribe your names:
That his own hand may strike his honour down,
That violates the smallest branch herein:
If you are arm'd to do, as sworn to do,
Subscribe to your deep oaths, and keep it too.
LONGAVILLE: I am resolv'd, 'tis but a three years' fast:
The mind shall banquet, though the body pine,
Fat paunches have lean pates: and dainty bits,
Make rich the ribs, but bankerout the wits.

DUMAIN: My loving Lord, Dumain is mortified,
   The grosser manner of these world's delights,
   He throws upon the gross world's baser slaves:
   To love, to wealth, to pomp, I pine and die,
   With all these living in Philosophy.
BEROWNE: I can but say their protestation over,
   So much, dear Liege, I have already sworn,
   That is, to live and study here three years.
   But there are other strict observances:
   As not to see a woman in that term,
   Which I hope well is not enrolled there.
   And one day in a week to touch no food:
   And but one meal on every day beside:
   The which I hope is not enrolled there.
   And then to sleep but three hours in the night,
   And not be seen to wink of all the day.
   When I was wont to think no harm all night,
   And make a dark night too of half the day:
   Which I hope well is not enrolled there.
   O, these are barren tasks, too hard to keep,
   Not to see ladies, study, fast, not sleep.
KING: Your oath is pass'd, to pass away from these.
BEROWNE: Let me say no my Liege, and if you please,
   I only swore to study with your Grace,
   And stay here in your Court for three years' space.
LONGAVILLE: You swore to that Berowne, and to the rest.
BEROWNE: By yea and nay sir, then I swore in jest.
   What is the end of study, let me know?
KING: Why that to know which else we should not know.
BEROWNE: Things hid and barr'd (you mean) from common sense.
KING: Ay, that is study's god-like recompense.
BEROWNE: Come on then, I will swear to study so,

To know the thing I am forbid to know:
As thus, to study where I well may dine,
When I to feast expressly am forbid.
Or study where to meet some Mistress fine,
When Mistresses from common sense are hid.
Or having sworn too hard a keeping oath,
Study to break it, and not break my troth.
If study's gain be thus, and this be so,
Study knows that which yet it doth not know:
Swear me to this, and I will ne'er say no.

KING: These be the stops that hinder study quite,
And train our intellects to vain delight.

BEROWNE: Why! all delights are vain, and that most vain
Which with pain purchas'd, doth inherit pain,
As painfully to pore upon a book,
To seek the light of truth, while truth the while
Doth falsely blind the eyesight of his look:
Light seeking light, doth light of light beguile:
So ere you find where light in darkness lies,
Your light grows dark by losing of your eyes.
Study me how to please the eye indeed,
By fixing it upon a fairer eye,
Who dazzling so, that eye shall be his heed,
And give him light that it was blinded by.
Study is like the heaven's glorious Sun,
That will not be deep search'd with saucy looks:
Small have continual plodders ever won,
Save base authority from others' books.
These earthly godfathers of heaven's lights,
That give a name to every fixed star,
Have no more profit of their shining nights,
Than those that walk and wot not what they are.
Too much to know, is to know naught but fame:

And every godfather can give a name.

KING: How well he's read, to reason against reading.

DUMAIN: Proceeded well, to stop all good proceeding.

LONGAVILLE: He weeds the corn, and still lets grow the weeding.

BEROWNE: The spring is near when green geese are a-breeding.

DUMAIN: How follows that?

BEROWNE: Fit in his place and time.

DUMAIN: In reason nothing.

BEROWNE: Something then in rhyme.

KING: Berowne is like an envious sneaping frost,
That bites the first-born infants of the Spring.

BEROWNE: Well, say I am, why should proud Summer boast,
Before the birds have any cause to sing?
Why should I joy in any abortive birth?
At Christmas I no more desire a rose,
Than wish a snow in May's newfangled shows:
But like of each thing that in season grows.
So you to study now it is too late,
That were to climb o'er the house to unlock the little gate.

KING: Well, sit you out: go home Berowne: adieu.

BEROWNE: No my good Lord, I have sworn to stay with you.
And though I have for barbarism spoke more,
Than for that angel knowledge you can say,
Yet confident I'll keep what I have sworn,
And bide the penance of each three years' day.
Give me the paper, let me read the same,
And to the strict'st decrees I'll write my name.

KING: How well this yielding rescues thee from shame.

BEROWNE: *Item.* That no woman shall come within a mile
  of my Court.

  Hath this been proclaimed?

LONGAVILLE: Four days ago.

BEROWNE: Let's see the penalty.

  On pain of losing her tongue.

  Who devis'd this penalty?

LONGAVILLE: Marry that did I.

BEROWNE: Sweet Lord, and why?

LONGAVILLE: To fright them hence with that dread
  penalty.

BEROWNE: A dangerous law against gentility.

  Item, If any man be seen to talk with a woman within the
  term of three years, he shall endure such public shame
  as the rest of the Court shall possibly devise.

  This Article my Liege yourself must break,

  For well you know here comes in embassy

  The French King's daughter, with yourself to speak:

  A maid of grace and complete majesty,

  About surrender up of Aquitaine

  To her decrepit, sick, and bedrid Father.

  Therefore this Article is made in vain,

  Or vainly comes th' admired Princess hither.

KING: What say you Lords?

  Why, this was quite forgot.

BEROWNE: So Study evermore is overshot,

  While it doth study to have what it would,

  It doth forget to do the thing it should:

  And when it hath the thing it hunteth most,

  'Tis won as towns with fire, so won, so lost.

KING. We must of force dispense with this decree.

  She must lie here on mere necessity.

BEROWNE: Necessity will make us all forsworn

Three thousand times within this three years' space:
For every man with his affects is born,
Not by might master'd, but by special grace.
If I break faith, this word shall speak for me,
I am forsworn on mere necessity.
So to the Laws at large I write my name,
And he that breaks them in the least degree,
Stands in attainder of eternal shame.
Suggestions are to other as to me:
But I believe although I seem so loath,
I am the last that will last keep his oath.
But is there no quick recreation granted?

KING: Ay that there is, our Court you know is haunted
With a refined traveller of Spain,
A man in all the world's new fashion planted,
That hath a mint of phrases in his brain:
One, who the music of his own vain tongue,
Doth ravish like enchanting harmony:
A man of complements whom right and wrong
Have chose as umpire of their mutiny.
This child of fancy that Armado hight,
For interim to our studies shall relate,
In high-born words the worth of many a Knight:
From tawny Spain lost in the world's debate.
How you delight my Lords, I know not I,
But I protest I love to hear him lie,
And I will use him for my minstrelsy.

BEROWNE: Armado is a most illustrious wight,
A man of fire, new words, fashion's own Knight.

LONGAVILLE: Costard the swain and he, shall be our sport,
And so to study, three years is but short.

Enter a Constable with Costard with a letter.

CONSTABLE: Which is the Duke's own person?

BEROWNE: This fellow, What wouldst?

CONSTABLE: I myself reprehend his own person, for I am his grace's tharborough: But I would see his own person in flesh and blood.

BEROWNE: This is he.

CONSTABLE: Signior Arme, Arme, commends you: There's villainy abroad, this letter will tell you more.

CLOWN: Sir the contempts thereof are as touching me.

KING: A letter from the magnificent Armado.

BEROWNE: How low soever the matter, I hope in God for high words.

LONGAVILLE: A high hope for a low heaven, God grant us patience.

BEROWNE: To hear, or forbear laughing.

LONGAVILLE: To hear meekly sir, and to laugh moderately, or to forbear both.

BEROWNE: Well sir, be it as the style shall give us cause to climb in the merriness.

CLOWN: The matter is to me sir, as concerning Jaquenetta. The matter of it is, I was taken with the manner.

BEROWNE: In what manner?

CLOWN: In manner and form following sir all those three. I was seen with her in the Manor house, sitting with her upon the form, and taken following her into the park: which put together, is in manner and form following. Now sir for the manner; It is the manner of a man to speak to a woman, for the form in some form.

BEROWNE: For the following sir.

CLOWN: As it shall follow in my correction, and God defend the right.

KING: Will you hear this letter with attention?

BEROWNE: As we would hear an Oracle.

CLOWN: Such is the simplicity of man to hearken after the flesh.

KING: *Great Deputy, the Welkin's Vicegerent, and sole dominator of Navarre, my soul's earth's god, and body's fostering patron.*

CLOWN: Not a word of Costard yet.

KING: *So it is.*

CLOWN: It may be so; but if he say it is so, he is in telling true; but so.

KING: Peace –

CLOWN: Be to me, and every man that dares not fight.

KING: No words –

CLOWN: Of other men's secrets I beseech you.

KING: *So it is besieged with sable-coloured melancholy, I did commend the black oppressing humour to the most wholesome physic of thy health-giving air: And as I am a Gentleman, betook myself to walk: The time When? About the sixth hour, when beasts most graze, birds best peck, and men sit down to that nourishment which is called supper. So much for the time When. Now for the ground Which? which I mean I walk'd upon, it is ycliped Thy Park. Then for the place Where? where I mean I did encounter that obscene and most preposterous event that draweth from my snow-white pen the ebon-coloured ink, which here thou viewest beholdest, surveyest, or seest. But to the place Where? It standeth North North-east and by East from the West corner of thy curious-knotted garden; There did I see that low-spirited swain, that base minnow of thy mirth –*

CLOWN: Me?

KING: *that unlettered small-knowing soul –*

CLOWN: Me?

KING: *that shallow vassal –*

CLOWN: Still me?

KING: *which, as I remember, hight Costard —*

CLOWN: O me!

KING: *sorted and consorted, contrary to thy established proclaimed edict and continent canon: Which with, O, with —
but with this I passion to say wherewith —*

CLOWN: With a wench.

KING: *with a child of our Grandmother Eve, a female; or for
thy more sweet understanding a woman: him I (as my ever-
esteemed duty pricks me on) have sent to thee, to receive the
meed of punishment by thy sweet Grace's officer Anthony
Dull, a man of good repute, carriage, bearing, and estimation.*

CONSTABLE: Me, an't shall please you? I am Anthony
Dull.

KING: *For Jaquenetta (so is the weaker vessel called) which I
apprehended with the aforesaid swain, I keeper her as a
vessel of thy Law's fury, and shall at the least of thy sweet
notice, bring her to trial. Thine in all compliments of devoted
and heartburning heat of duty.*

> *Don Adriano de Armado*

BEROWNE: This is not so well as I looked for, but the best
that ever I heard.

KING: Ay the best, for the worst. But sirrah, What say you
to this?

CLOWN: Sir I confess the wench.

KING: Did you hear the Proclamation?

CLOWN: I do confess much of the hearing it, but little of
the marking of it.

KING: It was proclaimed a year's imprisonment to be taken
with a wench.

CLOWN: I was taken with none sir, I was taken with a
damosel.

KING: Well, it was proclaimed damosel.

CLOWN: This was no damosel neither sir, she was a virgin.

KING: It is so varied too, for it was proclaimed virgin.

CLOWN: If it were, I deny her virginity: I was taken with a maid.

KING: This maid will not serve your turn sir.

CLOWN: This maid will serve my turn sir.

KING: Sir I will pronounce your sentence: You shall fast a week with bran and water.

CLOWN: I had rather pray a month with mutton and porridge.

KING: And Don Armado shall be your keeper.
My Lord Berowne, see him deliver'd o'er,
And go we Lords to put in practice that,
Which each to other hath so strongly sworn.

Exeunt King, Longaville, and Dumain.

BEROWNE: I'll lay my head to any good man's hat,
These oaths and laws will prove an idle scorn.
Sirrah, come on.

CLOWN: I suffer for the truth sir; for true it is, I was taken with Jaquenetta, and Jaquenetta is a true girl, and therefore welcome the sour cup of prosperity, affliction may one day smile again, and until then sit thee down sorrow.

Exeunt.

I. 2

Enter Armado and Moth his page.

BRAGGART: Boy, what sign is it when a man of great spirit grows melancholy?

BOY: A great sign sir, that he will look sad.

BRAGGART: Why? sadness is one and the selfsame thing dear imp.

BOY: No no, O Lord sir no.

BRAGGART: How canst thou part sadness and melancholy my tender Juvenal?

BOY: By a familiar demonstration of the working, my tough signeur.

BRAGGART: Why tough signeur? Why tough signeur?

BOY: Why tender Juvenal? Why tender Juvenal?

BRAGGART: I spoke it tender Juvenal, as a congruent epitheton, appertaining to thy young days, which we may nominate tender.

BOY: And I tough signeur, as an appertinent title to your old time, which we may name tough.

BRAGGART: Pretty and apt.

BOY: How mean you sir, I pretty, and my saying apt? or I apt, and my saying pretty?

BRAGGART: Thou pretty because little.

BOY: Little pretty, because little: wherefore apt?

BRAGGART: And therefore apt, because quick.

BOY: Speak you this in my praise, Master?

BRAGGART: In thy condign praise.

BOY: I will praise an eel with the same praise.

BRAGGART: What? that an eel is ingenuous.

BOY: That an eel is quick.

BRAGGART: I do say thou art quick in answers. Thou heat'st my blood.

BOY: I am answer'd sir.

BRAGGART: I love not to be cross'd.

BOY: He speaks the mere contrary, crosses love not him.

BRAGGART: I have promis'd to study three years with the Duke.

BOY: You may do it in an hour sir.

BRAGGART: Impossible.

BOY: How many is one thrice told?

BRAGGART: I am ill at reckning, it fits the spirit of a tapster.

BOY: You are a gentleman and a gamester sir.

BRAGGART: I confess both, they are both the varnish of a complete man.

BOY: Then I am sure you know how much the gross sum of deuce-ace amounts to.

BRAGGART: It doth amount to one more than two.

BOY: Which the base vulgar call three.

BRAGGART: True.

BOY: Why sir is this such a piece of study? Now here's three studied, ere ye'll thrice wink, and how easy it is to put years to the word three, and study three years in two words, the dancing horse will tell you.

BRAGGART: A most fine figure.

BOY: To prove you a cipher.

BRAGGART: I will hereupon confess I am in love; and as it is base for a soldier to love; so am I in love with a base wench. If drawing my sword against the humour of affection, would deliver me from the rebrobate thought of it, I would take Desire prisoner, and ransom him to any French courtier for a new devis'd courtesy. I think scorn to sigh, methinks I should out-swear Cupid. Comfort me Boy. What great men have been in love?

BOY: Hercules Master.

BRAGGART: Most sweet Hercules: more authority dear Boy, name more: and sweet my child let them be men of good repute and carriage.

BOY: Samson Master, he was a man of good carriage, great carriage: for he carried the town gates on his back like a porter: and he was in love.

BRAGGART: O well-knit Samson, strong jointed Samson; I do excel thee in my rapier, as much as thou didst me in carrying gates. I am in love too. Who was Samson's love my dear Moth?

BOY: A woman, Master.

BRAGGART: Of what complexion?

BOY: Of all the four, or the three, or the two, or one of the four.

BRAGGART: Tell me precisely of what complexion?

BOY: Of the sea-water green sir.

BRAGGART: Is that one of the four complexions?

BOY: As I have read sir, and the best of them too.

BRAGGART: Green indeed is the colour of lovers: but to have a love of that colour, methinks Samson had small reason for it. He surely affected her for her wit.

BOY: It was so sir, for she had a green wit.

BRAGGART: My Love is most immaculate white and red.

BOY: Most immaculate thoughts Master, are masked under such colours.

BRAGGART: Define, define, well educated infant.

BOY: My father's wit, and my mother's tongue assist me.

BRAGGART: Sweet invocation of a child, most pretty and pathetical.

BOY: If she be made of white and red,
Her faults will ne'er be known:
For blushing cheeks by faults are bred,
And fears by pale white shown:
Then if she fear, or be to blame,
By this you shall not know,
For still her cheeks possess the same,
Which native she doth owe.

A dangerous rhyme master against the reason of white and red.

BRAGGART: Is there not a ballad Boy, of the King and the Beggar?

BOY: The world was very guilty of such a ballad some three ages since, but I think now 'tis not to be found:

B

or if it were, it would neither serve for the writing, nor
the tune.

BRAGGART: I will have that subject newly writ o'er, that I
may example my digression by some mighty precedent.
Boy, I do love that country girl that I took in the Park
with the rational hind Costard: she deserves well.

BOY: To be whipp'd: and yet a better love than my
Master.

BRAGGART: Sing Boy, my spirit grows heavy in love.

BOY: And that's great marvel, loving a light wench.

BRAGGART: I say sing.

BOY: Forbear till this company be past.

Enter Clown, Constable, and Wench.

CONSTABLE: Sir, the Duke's pleasure, is that you keep
Costard safe, and you must let him to take no delight,
nor no penance, but he must fast three days a week:
for this damsel, I must keep her at the Park, she is allowed
for the day-woman. Fare you well.

Exit.

BRAGGART: I do betray myself with blushing Maid.

MAID: Man.

BRAGGART: I will visit thee at the Lodge.

MAID: That's here by.

BRAGGART: I know where it is situate.

MAID: Lord how wise you are!

BRAGGART: I will tell thee wonders.

MAID: With what face?

BRAGGART: I love thee.

MAID: So I heard you say.

BRAGGART: And so farewell.

MAID: Fair weather after you.

CONSTABLE: Come Jaquenetta, away.

Exeunt.

BRAGGART: Villain, thou shalt fast for thy offences ere thou be pardoned.

CLOWN: Well sir, I hope when I do it, I shall do it on a full stomach.

BRAGGART: Thou shalt be heavily punished.

CLOWN: I am more bound to you than your fellows, for they are but lightly rewarded.

BRAGGART: Take away this villain, shut him up.

BOY: Come you transgressing slave, away.

CLOWN: Let me not be pent up sir, I will fast being loose.

BOY: No sir, that were fast and loose: thou shalt to prison.

CLOWN: Well, if ever I do see the merry days of desolation that I have seen, some shall see.

BOY: What shall some see?

CLOWN: Nay nothing, Master Moth, but what they look upon. It is not for prisoners to be silent in their words, and therefore I will say nothing: I thank God, I have as little patience as another man, and therefore I can be quiet.

Exeunt Boy and Clown.

BRAGGART: I do affect the very ground (which is base) where her shoe (which is baser) guided by her foot (which is basest) doth tread. I shall be forsworn (which is a great argument of falsehood) if I love. And how can that be true love, which is falsely attempted? Love is a familiar, Love is a Devil. There is no evil Angel but Love, yet was Samson so tempted, and he had an excellent strength: Yet was Salomon so seduced, and he had a very good wit. Cupid's butt shaft is too hard for Hercules' club, and therefore too much odds for a Spaniard's rapier: The first and second cause will not serve my turn: the passado he respects not, the duello he regards not; his disgrace is to be called boy, but his glory

is to subdue men. Adieu Valour, rust rapier, be still
drum, for your manager is in love; yea he loveth.
Assist me some extemporal god of rhyme, for I am sure I
shall turn sonnet. Devise Wit, write pen, for I am for
whole volumes in folio.

Exit.

II. 1

Enter the Princess of France, with three attending Ladies
(Rosaline, Maria, and Katharine) and three Lords
(one of them Boyet).

BOYET: Now Madam summon up your dearest spirits,
Consider who the King your father sends:
To whom he sends, and what's his embassy.
Yourself, held precious in the world's esteem,
To parley with the sole inheritor
Of all perfections that a man may owe,
Matchless Navarre, the plea of no less weight
Than Aquitaine, a dowry for a Queen.
Be now as prodigal of all dear grace,
As Nature was in making graces dear,
When she did starve the general world beside,
And prodigally gave them all to you.
PRINCESS: Good Lord Boyet, my beauty though but
  mean,
Needs not the painted flourish of your praise:
Beauty is bought by judgement of the eye,
Not uttered by base sale of chapmen's tongues:
I am less proud to hear you tell my worth,
Than you much willing to be counted wise,
In spending your wit in the praise of mine.
But now to task the tasker, good Boyet,

You are not ignorant, all-telling fame
Doth noise abroad Navarre hath made a vow,
Till painful study shall outwear three years,
No woman may approach his silent Court:
Therefore to's seemeth it a needful course,
Before we enter his forbidden gates,
To know his pleasure, and in that behalf
Bold of your worthiness, we single you,
As our best moving fair soliciter:
Tell him, the daughter of the King of France,
On serious business craving quick dispatch,
Importunes personal conference with his grace.
Haste, signify so much while we attend,
Like humble visag'd suitors his high will.

BOYET: Proud of employment, willingly I go.

Exit.

PRINCESS: All pride is willing pride, and yours is so:
Who are the Votaries my loving Lords,
That are vow fellows with this virtuous Duke?

LORD: Longaville is one.

PRINCESS: Know you the man?

MARIA: I know him Madam, at a marriage feast,
Between Lord Perigort and the beauteous heir
Of Jaques Falconbridge solemnized.
In Normandy saw I this Longaville,
A man of sovereign parts he is esteemed:
Well fitted in arts, glorious in arms:
Nothing becomes him ill that he would well.
The only soil of his fair virtue's gloss,
If virtue's gloss will stain with any soil,
Is a sharp wit match'd with too blunt a will:
Whose edge hath power to cut, whose will still wills,
It should none spare that come within his power.

PRINCESS: Some merry mocking Lord belike, is't so?

MARIA: They say so most, that most his humours know.

PRINCESS: Such short liv'd wits do wither as they grow.
Who are the rest?

KATHARINE: The young Dumain, a well accomplish'd
youth,
Of all that Virtue love, for virtue loved.
Most power to do most harm, least knowing ill;
For he hath wit to make an ill shape good,
And shape to win grace though she had no wit.
I saw him at the Duke Alençon's once,
And much too little of that good I saw,
Is my report to his great worthiness.

ROSALINE: Another of these students at that time,
Was there with him, as I have heard a truth.
Berowne they call him, but a merrier man,
Within the limit of becoming mirth,
I never spent an hour's talk withal.
His eye begets occasion for his wit,
For every object that the one doth catch,
The other turns to a mirth-moving jest,
Which his fair tongue (conceit's expositor)
Delivers in such apt and gracious words,
That aged ears play truant at his tales,
And younger hearings are quite ravished.
So sweet and voluble is his discourse.

PRINCESS: God bless my Ladies, are they all in love?
That every one her own hath garnished,
With such bedecking ornaments of praise.

MARIA: Here comes Boyet.

Enter Boyet.

PRINCESS: Now, what admittance Lord?

BOYET: Navarre had notice of your fair approach;

And he and his competitors in oath,
Were all address'd to meet you gentle Lady
Before I came: Marry thus much I have learnt,
He rather means to lodge you in the field,
Like one that comes here to besiege his Court,
Than seek a dispensation for his oath:
To let you enter his unpeopled house.
   Enter King, Longaville, Dumain, and Berowne.
Here comes Navarre.

KING: Fair Princess, welcome to the Court of Navarre.

PRINCESS: Fair I give you back again, and welcome I have
 not yet: the roof of this Court is too high to be yours,
 and welcome to the wide fields, too base to be mine.

KING: You shall be welcome Madam to my Court.

PRINCESS: I will be welcome then. Conduct me thither.

KING: Hear me dear Lady, I have sworn an oath.

PRINCESS: Our Lady help my Lord, he'll be forsworn.

KING: Not for the world fair Madam, by my will.

PRINCESS: Why, will shall break it, will, and nothing else.

KING: Your Ladyship is ignorant what it is.

PRINCESS: Were my Lord so, his ignorance were wise,
 Where now his knowledge must prove ignorance.
 I hear your grace hath sworn out housekeeping:
 'Tis deadly sin to keep that oath my Lord,
 And sin to break it:
 But pardon me, I am too sudden-bold,
 To teach a teacher ill beseemeth me.
 Vouchsafe to read the purpose of my coming,
 And suddenly resolve me in my suit.

KING: Madam, I will, if suddenly I may.

PRINCESS: You will the sooner that I were away,
 For you'll prove perjur'd if you make me stay.

BEROWNE: Did not I dance with you in Brabant once?

ROSALINE: Did not I dance with you in Brabant once?

BEROWNE: I know you did.

ROSALINE: How needless was it then to ask the question?

BEROWNE: You must not be so quick.

ROSALINE: 'Tis 'long of you that spur me with such questions.

BEROWNE: You wit's too hot, it speeds too fast, 'twill tire.

ROSALINE: Not till it leave the rider in the mire.

BEROWNE: What time a' day?

ROSALINE: The hour that fools should ask.

BEROWNE: Now fair befall your mask.

ROSALINE: Fair fall the face it covers.

BEROWNE: And send you many lovers.

ROSALINE: Amen, so you be none.

BEROWNE: Nay then will I be gone.

KING: Madam, your father here doth intimate,
The payment of a hundred thousand crowns,
Being but th' one half, of an entire sum,
Disbursed by my father in his wars.
But say that he, or we, as neither have
Receiv'd that sum; yet there remains unpaid
A hundred thousand more: in surety of the which,
One part of Aquitaine is bound to us,
Although not valued to the money's worth.
If then the King your father will restore
But that one half which is unsatisfied,
We will give up our right in Aquitaine,
And hold fair friendship with His Majesty:
But that it seems he little purposeth,
For here he doth demand to have repaid,
A hundred thousand crowns, and not demands
On payment of a hundred thousand crowns,
To have his title live in Aquitaine.

Which we much rather had depart withal,
And have the money by our father lent,
Than Aquitaine, so gelded as it is.
Dear Princess, were not his requests so far
From reason's yielding, your fair self should make
A yielding 'gainst some reason in my breast,
And go well satisfied to France again.

PRINCESS: You do the King my father too much wrong,
And wrong the reputation of your name,
In so unseeming to confess receipt
Of that which hath so faithfully been paid.

KING: I do protest I never heard of it,
And if you prove it, I'll repay it back,
Or yield up Aquitaine.

PRINCESS: We arrest your word:
Boyet, you can produce acquittances
For such a sum, from special officers,
Of Charles his father.

KING: Satisfy me so.

BOYET: So please your Grace, the packet is not come.
Where that and other specialties are bound,
Tomorrow you shall have a sight of them.

KING: It shall suffice me; at which interview
All liberal reason I will yield unto:
Meantime receive such welcome at my hand,
As Honour, without breach of honour may
Make tender of, to thy true worthiness.
You may not come fair Princess in my gates,
But here without you shall be so receiv'd,
As you shall deem yourself lodg'd in my heart,
Though so deni'd farther harbour in my house:
Your own good thoughts excuse me, and farewell,
Tomorrow shall we visit you again.

PRINCESS: Sweet health and fair desires consort your grace.

KING: Thy own wish wish I thee, in every place.

Exit.

BEROWNE: Lady, I will commend you to my own heart.

ROSALINE: Pray you do my commendations,
I would be glad to see it.

BEROWNE: I would you heard it groan.

ROSALINE: Is the soul sick?

BEROWNE: Sick at the heart.

ROSALINE: Alack, let it blood.

BEROWNE: Would that do it good?

ROSALINE: My physic says ay.

BEROWNE: Will you prick't with your eye?

ROSALINE: No point, with my knife.

BEROWNE: Now God save thy life.

ROSALINE: And yours from long living.

BEROWNE: I cannot stay thanks-giving.

Exit.
Enter Dumain.

DUMAIN: Sir, I pray you a word: What Lady is that same?

BOYET: The heir of Alençon, Katharine her name.

DUMAIN: A gallant Lady, Mounsieur fare you well.

Exit.

LONGAVILLE: I beseech you a word: What is she in the white?

BOYET: A woman sometimes, if you saw her in the light.

LONGAVILLE: Perchance light in the light: I desire her name.

BOYET: She hath but one for herself,
To desire that were a shame.

LONGAVILLE: Pray you sir, whose daughter?

BOYET: Her mother's, I have heard.

LONGAVILLE: God's blessing an your beard.

BOYET: Good sir be not offended,
  She is an heir of Falconbridge.

LONGAVILLE: Nay, my choler is ended:
  She is a most sweet lady.

BOYET: Not unlike sir, that may be.

Exit Longaville.

Enter Berowne.

BEROWNE: What's her name in the cap?

BOYET: Rosaline by good hap.

BEROWNE: Is she wedded, or no?

BOYET: To her will sir, or so.

BEROWNE: You are welcome sir, adieu.

BOYET: Farewell to me sir, and welcome to you.

Exit Berowne.

MARIA: That last is Berowne, the merry madcap Lord.
  Not a word with him, but a jest.

BOYET: And every jest but a word.

PRINCESS: It was well done of you to take him at his word.

BOYET: I was as willing to grapple, as he was to board.

MARIA: Two hot sheeps marry:
  And wherefore not ships?

BOYET: No sheep (sweet lamb) unless we feed on your lips.

MARIA: You sheep and I pasture: shall that finish the jest?

BOYET: So you grant pasture for me.

MARIA: Not so gentle beast.
  My lips are no common, though several they be.

BOYET: Belonging to whom?

MARIA: To my fortunes and me.

PRINCESS: Good wits will be jangling, but gentles agree.
  This civil war of wits were much better used
  On Navarre and his bookmen, for here 'tis abused.

BOYET: If my observation (which very seldom lies

By the heart's still rhetoric, disclosed with eyes)
Deceive me not now, Navarre is infected.

PRINCESS: With what?

BOYET: With that which we lovers entitle affected.

PRINCESS: Your reason.

BOYET: Why all his behaviours do make their retire,
To the court of his eye, peeping thorough desire:
His heart like an agot with your print impressed,
Proud with his form, in his eye pride expressed.
His tongue all impatient to speak and not see,
Did stumble with haste in his eyesight to be,
All senses to that sense did make their repair,
To feel only looking on fairest of fair:
Me thought all his senses were lock'd in his eye,
As jewels in crystal for some Prince to buy
Who tendering their own worth from where they were
    glass'd,
Did point out to buy them along as you pass'd.
His face's own margent did coat such amazes,
That all eyes saw his eyes enchanted with gazes.
I'll give you Aquitaine, and all that is his,
And you give him for my sake, but one loving kiss.

PRINCESS: Come to our pavilion, Boyet is dispos'd.

BOYET: But to speak that in words, which his eye hath
    disclos'd.
I only have made a mouth of his eye,
By adding a tongue, which I know will not lie.

ROSALINE: Thou art an old love-monger, and speakest
    skillfully.

MARIA: He is Cupid's grandfather, and learns news of him.

ROSALINE: Then was Venus like her mother, for her father
    is but grim.

BOYET: Do you hear my mad wenches?

MARIA: No.

BOYET: What then, do you see?

ROSALINE: Ay, our way to be gone.

BOYET: You are too hard for me.

Exeunt.

III. 1

Enter Braggart and Boy.
Song.

BRAGGART: Warble child, make passionate my sense of hearing.

BOY: Concolinel.

BRAGGART: Sweet air, go tenderness of years: take this key, give enlargement to the swain, bring him festinately hither: I must employ him in a letter to my Love.

BOY: Will you win your love with a French brawl?

BRAGGART: How meanest thou, brawling in French?

BOY: No my complete master, but to jig off a tune at the tongue's end, canary to it with the feet, humour it with turning up your eye: sigh a note and sing a note, sometime through the throat: as if you swallow'd love with singing love, sometime through the nose as if you snuff'd up love by smelling love with your hat penthouse-like o'er the shop of your eyes, with your arms cross'd on your thinbelly doublet, like a rabbit on a spit, or your hands in your pocket, like a man after the old painting, and keep not too long in one tune, but a snip and away: these are complements, these are humours, these betray nice wenches that would be betrayed without these, and make them men of note: do you note men that most are affected to these?

BRAGGART: How hast thou purchased this experience?

BOY: By my penny of observation.

BRAGGART: But O, but O.

BOY: The hobbyhorse is forgot.

BRAGGART: Call'st thou my love hobbyhorse?

BOY: No Master, the hobbyhorse is but a colt, and your love perhaps, a hackney:

But have you forgot your Love?

BRAGGART: Almost I had.

BOY: Negligent student, learn her by heart.

BRAGGART: By heart, and in heart, Boy.

BOY: And out of heart, Master: all those three I will prove.

BRAGGART: What wilt thou prove?

BOY: A man, if I live (and this) by, in, and without, upon the instant: by heart you love her, because your heart cannot come by her: in heart you love her, because your heart is in love with her: and out of heart you love her, being out of heart that you cannot enjoy her.

BRAGGART: I am all these three.

BOY: And three times as much more, and yet nothing at all.

BRAGGART: Fetch hither the swain, he must carry me a letter.

BOY: A message well sympathiz'd, a horse to be ambassador for an ass.

BRAGGART: Ha, ha, What sayest thou?

BOY: Marry sir, you must send the ass upon the horse for he is very slow-gaited: but I go.

BRAGGART: The way is but short, away.

BOY: As swift as lead sir.

BRAGGART: Thy meaning pretty ingenious, is not lead a metal heavy, dull, and slow?

BOY: *Minime* honest Master, or rather Master no.

BRAGGART: I say lead is slow.

BOY: You are too swift sir to say so. Is that lead slow which is fir'd from a gun?

BRAGGART: Sweet smoke of rhetoric,
He reputes me a cannon, and the bullet that's he:
I shoot thee at the swain.

BOY: Thump then, and I flee.

Exit.

BRAGGART: A most acute juvenal, voluble and free of grace,
By the favour sweet welkin, I must sigh in thy face.
Most rude melancholy, Valour gives thee place.
My herald is return'd.

Enter Boy with Clown.

BOY: A wonder Master, here's a Costard broken in a shin.

BRAGGART: Some enigma, some riddle, come, thy l'envoy begin.

CLOWN: No egma, no riddle, no l'envoy, no salve, in the mail sir. Or sir, plantan, a plain plantan: no l'envoy, no l'envoy, no salve sir, but a plantan.

BRAGGART: By virtue thou enforcest laughter, thy silly thought, my spleen, the heaving of my lungs provokes me to ridiculous smiling: O pardon me my stars, doth the inconsiderate take *salve* for *l'envoy* and the word *l'envoy* for a *salve*?

BOY: Do the wise think them other, is not *l'envoy* a *salve*?

BRAGGART: No Page, it is an epilogue or discourse to make plain,
Some obscure precedence that hath tofore been sain.
[I will example it:
    The fox, the ape, and the humblebee
    Were still at odds, being but three.
There's the moral. Now the l'envoy.

BOY: I will add the l'envoy. Say the moral again.

BRAGGART: The fox, the ape, the humblebee
           Were still at odds, being but three.

BOY: Until the goose came out of door,
      And stayed the odds by adding four.]

  Now will I begin your moral, and do you follow with
  my l'envoy.

          The Fox, the Ape, and the Humblebee,
          Were still at odds, being but three.

BRAGGART: Until the Goose came out of door,
          Staying the odds by adding four.

BOY: A good l'envoy, ending in the Goose: would you
  desire more?

CLOWN: The Boy hath sold him a bargain, a Goose, that's
  flat.

  Sir, your pennyworth is good, and your goose be fat.
  To sell a bargain well is as cunning as fast and loose:
  Let me see a fat l'envoy, ay that's a fat Goose.

BRAGGART: Come hither, come hither:
  How did this argument begin?

BOY: By saying that a Costard was broken in a shin.
  Then call'd you for the l'envoy.

CLOWN: True, and I for a plantan:
  Thus came your argument in:
  Then the boy's fat l'envoy, the Goose that you bought,
  And he ended the market.

BRAGGART: But tell me: How was there a Costard broken
  in a shin?

BOY: I will tell you sensibly.

CLOWN: Thou hast no feeling of it Moth,
  I will speak that l'envoy.
  I Costard running out, that was safely within,
  Fell over the threshold, and broke my shin.

BRAGGART: We will talk no more of this matter.

CLOWN: Till there be more matter in the shin.

BRAGGART: Sirrah Costard, I will enfranchise thee.

CLOWN: O, marry me to one Frances, I smell some l'envoy, some Goose in this.

BRAGGART: By my sweet soul, I mean, setting thee at liberty, Enfreedoming thy person: thou wert immured, restrained, captivated, bound.

CLOWN: True, true, and now you will be my purgation, and let me loose.

BRAGGART: I give thee thy liberty, set thee from durance, and in lieu thereof, impose on thee nothing but this: Bear this significant to the country maid Jaquenetta: there is remuneration, for the best ward of mine honour is rewarding my dependents. Moth, follow.

Exit.

BOY: Like the sequel, I.
Signor Costard adieu.

Exit.

CLOWN: My sweet ounce of man's flesh, my incony Jew: Now will I look to his remuneration. Remuneration. O, that's the Latin word for three-farthings: Three farthings remuneration, What's the price of this inkle? 1d, no, I'll give you a remuneration: Why? It carries it remuneration: Why? It is a fairer name than French crown. I will never buy and sell out of this word.

Enter Berowne.

BEROWNE: O my good knave Costard, exceedingly well met.

CLOWN: Pray you sir. How much carnation ribbon may a man buy for a remuneration?

BEROWNE: What is a remuneration?

CLOWN: Marry sir, halfpenny farthing.

BEROWNE: O, Why then, three-farthings worth of silk.

CLOWN: I thank your worship, God be wi' you.

BEROWNE: O stay slave, I must employ thee:
   As thou wilt win my favour, good my knave,
   Do one thing for me that I shall entreat.

CLOWN: When would you have it done sir?

BEROWNE: O this afternoon.

CLOWN: Well, I will do it sir: Fare you well.

BEROWNE: O thou knowest not what it is.

CLOWN: I shall know sir, when I have done it.

BEROWNE: Why villain thou must know first.

CLOWN: I will come to your worship tomorrow morning.

BEROWNE: It must be done this afternoon,
   Hark slave, it is but this:
   The Princess comes to hunt here in the Park,
   And in her train there is a gentle Lady:
   When tongues speak sweetly, then they name her name,
   And Rosaline they call her, ask for her:
   And to her white hand see thou do commend
   This seal'd-up counsel. There's thy guerdon: go.

CLOWN: Gardon, O sweet gardon, better than remuneration, a 'levenpence farthing better: most sweet gardon.
   I will do it sir in print: gardon, remuneration.

Exit.

BEROWNE: O, and I forsooth, in love:
   I that have been love's whip?
   A very Beadle to a humorous sigh,
   A critic, nay, a night-watch constable,
   A domineering pedant o'er the Boy,
   Than whom no mortal so magnificent.
   This wimpled, whining, purblind wayward Boy,
   This senior-junior giant dwarf, Don Cupid,
   Regent of love-rhymes, Lord of folded arms,

The anointed sovereign of sighs and groans:
Liege of all loiterers and malcontents:
Dread Prince of plackets, King of codpieces,
Sole Imperator and great general
Of trotting paritors (O my little heart.)
And I to be a Corporal of his field,
And wear his colours like a tumbler's hoop.
What? I love, I sue, I seek a wife,
A woman that is like a German clock,
Still a-repairing: ever out of frame,
And never going aright, being a watch:
But being watch'd, that it may still go right.
Nay, to be perjur'd, which is worst of all:
And among three, to love the worst of all,
A whitely wanton, with a velvet brow.
With two pitch balls stuck in her face for eyes.
Ay, and by heaven, one that will do the deed,
Though Argus were her eunuch and her guard.
And I to sigh for her, to watch for her,
To pray for her, go to: it is a plague
That Cupid will impose for my neglect,
Of his almighty dreadful little might.
Well, I will love, write, sigh, pray, sue, groan.
Some men must love my Lady, and some Joan.
                    Exit.

IV. 1

Enter the Princess, a Forester, her Ladies and her Lords.

PRINCESS: Was that the King that spurr'd his horse so hard,
  Against the steep uprising of the hill?

BOYET: I know not, but I think it was not he.

PRINCESS: Whoe'er a' was, a' showed a mounting mind:

Well Lords, today we shall have our dispatch,
On Saturday we will return to France.
Then forester my friend, where is the bush
That we must stand and play the murtherer in?

FORESTER: Hereby upon the edge of yonder coppice,
A stand where you may make the fairest shoot.

PRINCESS: I thank my beauty, I am fair that shoot,
And thereupon thou speak'st the fairest shoot.

FORESTER: Pardon me Madam, for I meant not so.

PRINCESS: What, what? First praise me, and then again
 say no.
O short liv'd pride. Not fair? alack for woe.

FORESTER: Yes Madam fair.

PRINCESS: Nay, never paint me now,
Where fair is not, praise cannot mend the brow.
Here (good my glass) take this for telling true:
Fair payment for foul words, is more than due.

FORESTER: Nothing but fair is that which you inherit.

PRINCESS: See, see, my beauty will be sav'd by merit.
O heresy in fair, fit for these days,
A giving hand, though foul, shall have fair praise.
But come, the bow: Now mercy goes to kill,
And shooting well, is then accounted ill:
Thus will I save my credit in the shoot,
Not wounding, pity would not let me do't:
If wounding, then it was to show my skill,
That more for praise, than purpose meant to kill.
And out of question, so it is sometimes:
Glory grows guilty of detested crimes,
When for Fame's sake, for praise an outward part,
We bend to that, the working of the heart.
As I for praise alone now seek to spill
The poor deer's blood, that my heart means no ill.

BOYET: Do not curst wives hold that self-sovereignty
    Only for praise sake, when they strive to be
    Lords o'er their Lords?
PRINCESS: Only for praise, and praise we may afford,
    To any Lady that subdues a Lord.
                    Enter Clown.
BOYET: Here comes a member of the commonwealth.
CLOWN: God dig-you-den all, pray you which is the head
    Lady?
PRINCESS: Thou shalt know her fellow, by the rest that
    have no heads.
CLOWN: Which is the greatest Lady, the highest?
PRINCESS: The thickest, and the tallest.
CLOWN: The thickest, and the tallest: it is so, truth is truth.
    And your waist Mistress, were as slender as my wit,
    One o' these maids' girdles for your waist should be fit.
    Are not you the chief woman? You are the thickest here?
PRINCESS: What's your will sir? What's your will?
CLOWN: I have a letter from Monsier Berowne,
    To one Lady Rosaline.
PRINCESS: O thy letter, thy letter: He's a good friend of
    mine.
    Stand aside good bearer.
    Boyet, you can carve,
    Break up this capon.
BOYET: I am bound to serve.
    This letter is mistook: it importeth none here:
    It is writ to Jaquenetta.
PRINCESS: We will read it, I swear.
    Break the neck of the wax, and everyone give ear.
BOYET *reads:* By heaven, that thou art fair, is most in-
    fallible: true that thou art beauteous, truth itself that
    thou art lovely: more fairer than fair, beautiful than

beauteous, truer than truth itself: have commiseration on thy heroical vassal. The magnanimous and most illustrate King Cophetua set eye upon the pernicious and indubitate beggar Zenelophon: and he it was that might rightly say, *Veni, vidi, vici*: Which to annothanize in the vulgar, O base and obscure vulgar; *videlicet*, He came, See, and overcame: he came one; see, two; overcame three: Who came? the King. Why did he come? to see. Why did he see? to overcome. To whom came he? to the beggar. What saw he? the beggar. Who overcame he? the beggar. The conclusion is victory: On whose side? the King's: the captive is enrich'd: On whose side? the beggar's. The catastrophe is a nuptial: on whose side? the King's: no, on both in one, or one in both. I am the King (for so stands the comparison) thou the beggar, for so witnesseth thy lowliness. Shall I command thy love? I may. Shall I enforce thy love? I could. Shall I entreat thy love? I will. What, shalt thou exchange for rags, robes: for tittles titles, for thyself me. Thus expecting thy reply, I profane my lips on thy foot, my eyes on thy picture, and my heart on thy every part.

Thine, in the dearest design of industry,
Don Adriano de Armatho.

Thus dost thou hear the Nemean Lion roar,
'Gainst thee thou Lamb, that standest as his prey:
Submissive fall his princely feet before,
And he from forage will incline to play.

But if thou strive (poor soul) what art thou then?
Food for his rage, repasture for his den.

PRINCESS: What plume of feathers is he that indited this letter?
What vane? What weathercock? Did you ever hear better?

BOYET: I am much deceived, but I remember the style.

PRINCESS: Else your memory is bad, going o'er it erewhile.

BOYET: This Armado is a Spaniard that keeps here in court
A Phantasime, a Monarcho, and one that makes sport
To the Prince and his book-mates.

PRINCESS: Thou fellow, a word. Who gave thee this letter?

CLOWN: I told you, my Lord.

PRINCESS: To whom shouldst thou give it?

CLOWN: From my Lord to my Lady.

PRINCESS: From which Lord, to which Lady?

CLOWN: From my Lord Berowne, a good master of mine,
To a Lady of France, that he call'd Rosaline.

PRINCESS: Thou hast mistaken his letter. Come Lords, away.
Here sweet, put up this, 'twill be thine another day.
Exit Princess.

BOYET: Who is the shooter? Who is the shooter?

ROSALINE: Shall I teach you to know?

BOYET: Ay my continent of beauty.

ROSALINE: Why she that bears the bow. Finely put off.

BOYET: My Lady goes to kill horns, but if thou marry,
Hang me by the neck, if horns that year miscarry.
Finely put on.

ROSALINE: Well then, I am the shooter.

BOYET: And who is your deer?

ROSALINE: If we choose by the horns, yourself come not near. Finely put on indeed.

MARIA: You still wrangle with her Boyet, and she strikes at the brow.

BOYET: But she herself is hit lower:
Have I hit her now?

ROSALINE: Shall I come upon thee with an old saying,
that was a man when King Pepin of France was a little
boy, as touching the hit it.

BOYET: So I may answer thee with one as old that was a
woman when Queen Guinever of Britain was a little
wench, as touching the hit it,

ROSALINE: Thou canst not hit it, hit it, hit it,
       Thou canst not hit it my good man.

BOYET: And I cannot, cannot, cannot:
       And I cannot, another can.
       Exeunt Rosaline and Katharine.

CLOWN: By my troth most pleasant, how both did fit it.

MARIA: A mark marvellous well shot, for they both did hit it.

BOYET: A mark, O mark but that mark: a mark says my
Lady.
Let the mark have a prick in't, to mete at, if it may be.

MARIA: Wide a' th' bow hand, yfaith your hand is out.

CLOWN: Indeed a' must shoot nearer, or he'll ne'er hit the
clout.

BOYET: And if my hand be out, then belike your hand is in.

CLOWN: Then will she get the upshoot by cleaving the pin.

MARIA: Come, come, you talk greasily, your lips grow foul.

CLOWN: She's too hard for you at pricks, sir challenge her
to bowl.

BOYET: I fear too much rubbing: good night my good Owl.
       Exeunt Boyet and Maria.

CLOWN: By my soul a swain, a most simple clown.
Lord, Lord, how the Ladies and I have put him down.
O' my troth most sweet jests, most incony vulgar wit,
When it comes so smoothly off, so obscenely, as it were,
so fit.
Armatho th' one side, O a most dainty man.
To see him walk before a Lady, and to bear her fan.

To see him kiss his hand, and how most sweetly a' will
    swear:
And his Page a' t'other side, that handful of wit,
Ah heavens, it is a most pathetical nit.
Sola, sola.

Exeunt.
Shout Within.

IV. 2

Enter Dull, Holofernes the Pedant, and Nathaniel the Curate.

CURATE: Very reverend sport truly, and done in the
    testimony of a good conscience.

PEDANT: The deer was (as you know) *sanguis* in blood,
    ripe as a pomewater, who now hangeth like a jewel in the
    ear of *caelo* the sky, the welkin the heaven, and anon falleth
    like a crab on the face of *terra,* the soil, the land, the earth.

CURATE: Truly M. Holofernes, the epithets are sweetly
    varied like a scholar at the least: but sir I assure ye, it was
    a buck of the first head.

PEDANT: Sir Nathaniel, *haud credo.*

CONSTABLE: 'Twas not a *haud credo,* 'twas a pricket.

PEDANT: Most barbarous intimation: yet a kind of insinu-
    ation, as it were *in via,* in way of explication *facere:* as it
    were replication, or rather *ostentare,* to show as it were
    his inclination after his undressed, unpolished, unedu-
    cated, unpruned, untrained, or rather unlettered, or
    ratherest unconfirmed fashion, to insert again my
    haud credo for a deer.

CONSTABLE: I said the deer was not a *haud credo,* 'twas a
    pricket.

PEDANT: Twice-sod simplicity, *bis coctus,* O thou monster
    Ignorance, how deformed dost thou look.

CURATE: Sir he hath never fed of the dainties that are bred in a book.

He hath not eat paper as it were;

He hath not drunk ink.

His intellect is not replenished, he is only an animal, only sensible in the duller parts: and such barren plants are set before us, that we thankful should be: which we of taste and feeling, are for those parts that do fructify in us more than he.

For as it would ill become me to be vain, indiscreet, or a fool;

So were there a patch set on Learning, to see him in a school.

[But *omne bene,* say I, being of an old father's mind,

Many can brook the weather that love not the wind.]

CONSTABLE: You two are bookmen: Can you tell me by your wit,

What was a month old at Cain's birth, that's not five weeks old as yet?

PEDANT: Dictynna goodman Dull, Dictynna goodman Dull.

CONSTABLE: What is Dictynna?

CURATE: A title to Phoebe, to Luna, to the Moon.

PEDANT: The moon was a month old when Adam was no more,

And raught not to five weeks when he came to five-score.

Th' allusion holds in the exchange.

CONSTABLE: 'Tis true indeed, the collusion holds in the exchange.

PEDANT: God comfort thy capacity, I say th' allusion holds in the exchange.

CONSTABLE: And I say the pollusion holds in the exchange: for the Moon is never but a month old: and I say beside that, 'twas a pricket that the Princess kill'd.

PEDANT: Sir Nathaniel, will you hear an extemporal Epitaph on the death of the deer, and to humour the ignorant call I the deer, the Princess kill'd a pricket.

CURATE: *Perge,* good M. Holofernes, *perge,* so it shall please you to abrogate scurrility.

PEDANT: I will something affect the letter, for it argues facility.

> *The prayfull Princess pierc'd and prick'd a pretty pleasing Pricket,*
> *Some say a Sore, but not a sore, till now made sore with shooting.*
> *The dogs did yell, put ell to Sore, then Sorel jumps from thicket:*
> *Or Pricket sore, or else Sorel, the people fall a hooting.*
> *If Sore be sore, then ell to Sore, makes fifty sores o' sorel:*
> *Of one sore I an hundred make by adding but one more L.*

CURATE: A rare talent.

CONSTABLE: If a talent be a claw, look how he claws him with a talent.

PEDANT: This is a gift that I have simple: simple, a foolish extravagant spirit, full of forms, figures, shapes, objects, ideas, apprehensions, motions, revolutions. These are begot in the ventricle of memory, nourish'd in the womb of pia mater, and deliver'd upon the mellowing of occasion: but the gift is good in those in whom it is acute, and I am thankful for it.

CURATE: Sir, I praise the Lord for you, and so may my parishioners, for their sons are well tutor'd by you, and their daughters profit very greatly under you: you are a good member of the commonwealth.

PEDANT: *Me hercle,* If their sons be ingenuous, they shall want no instruction: If their daughters be capable, I will put it to them. But *vir sapit qui pauca loquitur,* a soul feminine saluteth us.

Enter Jaquenetta and the Clown.

MAID: God give you good morrow M. Person.

PEDANT: Master Person, *quasi* Person? And if one should be perst, Which is the one?

CLOWN: Marry M. Schoolmaster, he that is likest to a hogshead.

PEDANT: Of persing a hogshead, a good lustre of conceit in a turf of earth, fire enough for a flint, pearl enough for a swine: 'tis pretty, it is well.

MAID: Good Master Parson, be so good as read me this letter, it was given me by Costard, and sent me from Don Armado. I beseech you read it.

PEDANT: *Fauste, precor gelida quando pecus omne sub umbra Ruminat –*

and so forth. Ah good old Mantuan, I may speak of thee as the traveller doth of Venice:

> *Venetia, Venetia,*
> *Chi non ti vede non ti pretia.*

Old Mantuan, old Mantuan. Who understandeth thee not, loves thee not. *Ut, re, sol, la, mi, fa:* Under pardon, sir, what are the contents? Or rather as Horace says in his – What my soul, verses?

CURATE: Ay sir, and very learned.

PEDANT: Let me hear a staff, a stanze, a verse. *Lege domine.*

CURATE: If Love make me forsworn, how shall I swear to love?

Ah never faith could hold, if not to beauty vowed.

Though to my self forsworn, to thee I'll faithful prove.

Those thoughts to me were oaks, to thee like osiers
   bowed.
Study his bias leaves, and makes his book thine eyes.
Where all those pleasures live, that Art would compre-
   hend.
If knowledge be the mark, to know thee shall suffice.
Well learned is that tongue, that well can thee commend,
All ignorant that soul, that sees thee without wonder.
Which is to me some praise, that I thy parts admire;
Thy eye Jove's lightning bears, thy voice his dreadful
   thunder.
Which not to anger bent, is music, and sweet fire.
Celestial as thou art, O pardon love this wrong,
That sings heaven's praise, with such an earthly tongue.

PEDANT: You find not the apostrophas, and so miss the
accent. Let me supervise the canzonet. Here are only
numbers ratified, but for the elegancy, facility, and
golden cadence of poesy *caret*: Ovidius Naso was the
man. And why in deed Naso, but for smelling out the
odoriferous flowers of fancy? the jerks of invention
imitari is nothing: So doth the hound his master, the ape
his keeper, the tired horse his rider: But damosella
virgin, Was this directed to you?

MAID: Ay sir, from one Mounsier Berowne, one of the
strange Queen's Lords.

PEDANT: I will overglance the superscript.
To the snow-white hand of the most beauteous Lady Rosaline.
I will look again on the intellect of the letter, for the nom-
ination of the party written to the person written unto:
Your Ladyship's in all desired employment, Berowne.

CURATE: Sir Holofernes, this Berowne is one of the
Votaries with the King, and here he hath framed a
letter to a sequent of the stranger Queen's: which

accidentally, or by the way of progression, hath mis-
carried. Trip and go my sweet, deliver this paper into the
royal hand of the King, it may concern much: stay not
thy compliment, I forgive thy duty, adieu.

MAID: Good Costard, go with me:
Sir God save your life.

CLOWN: Have with thee my girl.

Exeunt Clown and Jaquenetta.

CURATE: Sir you have done this in the fear of God very
religiously: and, as a certain Father saith –

PEDANT: Sir tell not me of the Father, I do fear colourable
colours. But to return to the verses, did they please you
Sir Nathaniel?

CURATE: Marvellous well for the pen.

PEDANT: I do dine today at the father's of a certain pupil of
mine, where if (being repast) it shall please you to gratify
the table with a Grace, I will on my privilege I have with
the parents of the foresaid child or pupil, undertake your
benvenuto, where I will prove those verses to be very
unlearned, neither savouring of poetry, wit, nor invention. I beseech your society.

CURATE: And thank you too: for society (saith the text) is
the happiness of life.

PEDANT: And certes the text most infallibly concludes it.
Sir I do invite you too, you shall not say me nay:
pauca verba.
Away, the gentles are at their game, and we will to our
recreation.

Exeunt.

IV. 3

Enter Berowne, with a paper in his hand, alone.

BEROWNE: The King he is hunting the deer,
I am coursing myself.
They have pitch'd a toil, I am toiling in a pitch, pitch that
defiles; defile, a foul word: Well, set thee down sorrow;
for so they say the fool said, and so say I, and I the fool:
Well proved wit. By the Lord this Love is as mad as
Ajax, it kills sheep, it kills me, I a sheep: Well proved
again a' my side. I will not love; if I do hang me; i'
faith I will not. O but her eye: by this light, but for her
eye, I would not love her; yes, for her two eyes. Well,
I do nothing in the world but lie, and lie in my throat.
By heaven I do love, and it hath taught me to rhyme, and
to be melancholy: and here is part of my rhyme, and
here my melancholy. Well, she hath one a' my Sonnets
already, the Clown bore it, the Fool sent it, and the
Lady hath it: sweet Clown, sweeter Fool, sweetest
Lady. By the world, I would not care a pin, if the other
three were in. Here comes one with a paper, God give
him grace to groan.

He stands aside. The King entereth.

KING: Ay me!

BEROWNE: Shot by heaven: proceed sweet Cupid, thou
hast thump'd him with thy bird bolt under the left
pap: in faith secrets.

KING: So sweet a kiss the golden Sun gives not,
To those fresh morning drops upon the rose,
As thy eye beams, when their fresh rays have smot
The night of dew that on my cheeks down flows.
Nor shines the silver Moon one half so bright,

Through the transparent bosom of the deep,
As doth thy face through tears of mine give light:
Thou shin'st in every tear that I do weep,
No drop, but as a coach doth carry thee:
So ridest thou triumphing in my woe.
Do but behold the tears that swell in me,
And they thy glory through my grief will show:
But do not love thyself, then thou wilt keep
My tears for glasses, and still make me weep.
O Queen of Queens, how far dost thou excel,
No thought can think, nor tongue of mortal tell.
How shall she know my griefs? I'll drop the paper.
Sweet leaves shade folly. Who is he comes here?

Enter Longaville. The King steps aside.

What Longaville, and reading: listen ear.

BEROWNE: Now in thy likeness, one more fool appear.

LONGAVILLE: Ay me, I am forsworn.

BEROWNE: Why he comes in like a perjure, wearing papers.

KING: In love I hope, sweet fellowship in shame.

BEROWNE: One drunkard loves another of the name.

LONGAVILLE: Am I the first that have been perjur'd so?

BEROWNE: I could put thee in comfort, not by two that I know,

Thou makest the triumviry, the cornercap of society,

The shape of Love's Tyburn, that hangs up simplicity.

LONGAVILLE: I fear these stubborn lines lack power to move.

O sweet Maria, Empress of my love,

These numbers will I tear, and write in prose.

BEROWNE: Oh, rhymes are guards on wanton Cupid's hose,

Disfigure not his slop.

LONGAVILLE: This same shall go.

He reads the Sonnet.

Did not the heavenly rhetoric of thine eye,
'Gainst whom the world cannot hold argument,
Persuade my heart to this false perjury?
Vows for thee broke deserve not punishment.
A woman I forswore, but I will prove,
Thou being a goddess, I forswore not thee.
My vow was earthly, thou a heavenly love.
Thy grace being gain'd, cures all disgrace in me.
Vows are but breath, and breath a vapour is.
Then thou fair Sun, which on my earth dost shine,
Exhalest this vapour-vow, in thee it is:
If broken then, it is no fault of mine:
If by me broke, what fool is not so wise,
To lose an oath, to win a Paradise?

BEROWNE: This is the liver vein, which makes flesh a deity.

A green goose, a goddess, pure pure idolatry.

God amend us, God amend, we are much out o' th' way.

Enter Dumain.

LONGAVILLE: By whom shall I send this – (company?) Stay.

BEROWNE: All hid, all hid, an old infant play,

Like a demi God, here sit I in the sky,

And wretched fools' secrets heedfully o'ereye.

More sacks to the mill. O heavens I have my wish,

Dumain transform'd, four woodcocks in a dish.

DUMAIN: O most divine Kate.

BEROWNE: O most profane coxcomb.

DUMAIN: By heaven the wonder of a mortal eye.

BEROWNE: By earth she is not, corporal, there you lie.

DUMAIN: Her amber hairs for foul hath amber coted.

c

BEROWNE: An amber coloured raven was well noted.

DUMAIN: As upright as the cedar.

BEROWNE: Stoop I say, her shoulder is with child.

DUMAIN: As fair as day.

BEROWNE: Ay as some days, but then no sun must shine.

DUMAIN: O that I had my wish!

LONGAVILLE: And I had mine.

KING: And I mine too good Lord.

BEROWNE: Amen, so I had mine: Is not that a good word?

DUMAIN: I would forget her, but a fever she
  Reigns in my blood, and will remember'd be.

BEROWNE: A fever in your blood, why then incision
  Would let her out in saucers, sweet misprision.

DUMAIN: Once more I'll read the Ode that I have writ.

BEROWNE: Once more I'll mark how Love can vary wit.

Dumain reads his Sonnet.

> *On a day, alack the day:*
> *Love, whose month is every May,*
> *Spied a blossom passing fair,*
> *Playing in the wanton air:*
> *Through the velvet, leaves the wind,*
> *All unseen, can passage find.*
> *That the lover sick to death,*
> *Wish himself the heaven's breath.*
> *Air (quoth he) thy cheeks may blow,*
> *Air, would I might triumph so.*
> *But alack my hand is sworn,*
> *Ne'er to pluck thee from thy thorn:*
> *Vow alack for youth unmeet,*
> *Youth so apt to pluck a sweet.*
> *Do not call it sin in me,*
> *That I am forsworn for thee.*
> *Thou for whom Jove would swear,*

Juno but an Ethiope were,
And deny himself for Jove,
Turning mortal for thy Love.

This will I send, and something else more plain.
That shall express my true-love's fasting pain.
O would the King, Berowne and Longaville,
Were lovers too, ill to example ill,
Would from my forehead wipe a perjur'd note:
For none offend, where all alike do dote.

LONGAVILLE: Dumain, thy Love is far from charity,
That in Love's grief desir'st society:
You may look pale, but I should blush I know,
To be o'erheard, and taken napping so.

KING: Come sir, you blush: as his, your case is such,
You chide at him, offending twice as much.
You do not love Maria? Longaville,
Did never Sonnet for her sake compile;
Nor never lay his wreathed arms athwart
His loving bosom, to keep down his heart.
I have been closely shrouded in this bush,
And mark'd you both, and for you both did blush.
I heard your guilty rhymes, observ'd your fashion:
Saw sighs reek from you, noted well your passion.
Aye me, says one! O Jove, the other cries!
One her hairs were gold, crystal the other's eyes.
You would for Paradise break faith and troth,
And Jove for your Love would infringe an oath.
What will Berowne say when that he shall hear
Faith infringed, which such zeal did swear.
How will he scorn? how will he spend his wit?
How will he triumph, leap, and laugh at it?
For all the wealth that ever I did see,
I would not have him know so much by me.

BEROWNE: Now step I forth to whip hypocrisy.
Ah good my Liege, I pray thee pardon me.
Good heart, What grace hast thou thus to reprove
These worms for loving, that art most in love?
Your eyes do make no coaches in your tears.
There is no certain Princess that appears.
You'll not be perjur'd, 'tis a hateful thing:
Tush, none but minstrels like of sonneting.
But are you not asham'd? nay, are you not
All three of you, to be thus much o'ershot?
You found his moth, the King your moth did see:
But I a beam do find in each of three.
O what a scene of foolery have I seen.
Of sighs, of groans, of sorrow, and of teen:
O me, with what strict patience have I sat,
To see a King transformed to a gnat?
To see great Hercules whipping a gig,
And profound Salomon tuning a jig,
And Nestor play at push-pin with the boys,
And Critic Timon laugh at idle toys.
Where lies thy grief? O tell me good Dumain;
And gentle Longaville, where lies thy pain?
And where my Liege's? all about the breast:
A caudle hoa!

KING: Too bitter is thy jest.
Are we betrayed thus to thy over-view?

BEROWNE: Not you to me, but I betrayed to you.
I that am honest I, that hold it sin
To break the vow I am engaged in.
I am betrayed by keeping company
With men like you, men of inconstancy.
When shall you see me write a thing in rhyme?
Or groan for Joan? or spend a minute's time,

In pruning me, when shall you hear that I
Will praise a hand, a foot, a face, an eye:
A gait, a state, a brow, a breast, a waist,
A leg, a limb.

KING: Soft, Whither away so fast?
A true man, or a thief, that gallops so.

BEROWNE: I post from Love, good lover let me go.

Enter Jaquenetta and Clown.

MAID: God bless the King.

KING: What present hast thou there?

CLOWN: Some certain treason.

KING: What makes treason here?

CLOWN: Nay it makes nothing sir.

KING: If it mar nothing neither,
The treason and you go in peace away together.

MAID: I beseech your Grace let this letter be read,
Our parson misdoubts it: it was treason he said.

KING: Berowne, read it over.

He reads the letter.

Where hadst thou it?

MAID: Of Costard.

KING: Where hadst thou it?

CLOWN: Of Dun Adramadio, Dun Adramadio.

KING: How now, what is in you? why dost thou tear it?

BEROWNE: A toy my Liege, a toy: your Grace needs not
fear it.

LONGAVILLE: It did move him to passion, and therefore
let's hear it.

DUMAIN: It is Berowne's writing, and here is his name.

BEROWNE: Ah you whoreson loggerhead, you were born
to do me shame.

Guilty my Lord, guilty: I confess, I confess.

KING: What?

BEROWNE: That you three fools lack'd me fool, to make
    up the mess.
  He, he, and you: and you my Liege, and I,
  Are pick-purses in Love, and we deserve to die.
  O dismiss this audience, and I shall tell you more.

DUMAIN: Now the number is even.

BEROWNE: True true, we are four: will these turtles be
    gone?

KING: Hence sirs, away.

CLOWN: Walk aside the true folk, and let the traitors stay.
        Exeunt Costard and Jaquenetta.

BEROWNE: Sweet Lords, sweet Lovers, O let us embrace,
  As true we are as flesh and blood can be,
  The sea will ebb and flow, heaven will show his face:
  Young blood doth not obey an old decree.
  We cannot cross the cause why we were born:
  Therefore of all hands must we be forsworn.

KING: What, did these rent lines show some love of thine?

BEROWNE: Did they, quoth you? Who sees the heavenly
    Rosaline,
  That (like a rude and savage man of Ind)
  At the first opening of the gorgeous East,
  Bows not his vassal head, and strooken blind,
  Kisses the base ground with obedient breast?
  What peremptory eagle-sighted eye
  Dares look upon the heaven of her brow,
  That is not blinded by her majesty?

KING: What zeal, what fury, hath inspir'd thee now?
  My Love (her Mistress) is a gracious Moon,
  She (an attending star) scarce seen a light.

BEROWNE: My eyes are then no eyes, nor I Berowne.
  O, but for my Love, day would turn to night,
  Of all complexions the cull'd sovereignty,

Do meet as at a fair in her fair cheek,
Where several Worthies make one dignity,
Where nothing wants, that want itself doth seek.
Lend me the flourish of all gentle tongues,
Fie painted Rhetoric, O she needs it not.
To things of sale, a seller's praise belongs:
She passes praise, then praise too short doth blot.
A withered hermit, fivescore winters worn,
Might shake off fifty, looking in her eye:
Beauty doth varnish Age, as if new born,
And gives the crutch the cradle's infancy.
O 'tis the Sun that maketh all things shine.

KING: By heaven, thy Love is black as ebony.

BEROWNE: Is ebony like her? O wood divine!
A wife of such wood were felicity.
O who can give an oath? Where is a book?
That I may swear Beauty doth beauty lack,
If that she learn not of her eye to look:
No face is fair that is not full so black.

KING: O paradox, Black is the badge of hell,
The hue of dungeons, and the School of night:
And beauty's crest becomes the heavens well.

BEROWNE: Devils soonest tempt resembling spirits of light.
O if in black my Lady's brows be deck'd,
It mourns, that painting and usurping hair
Should ravish doters with a false aspect:
And therefore is she born to make black, fair.
Her favour turns the fashion of the days,
For native blood is counted painting now:
And therefore red that would avoid dispraise,
Paints itself black, to imitate her brow.

DUMAIN: To look like her are chimney-sweepers black.

LONGAVILLE: And since her time, are colliers counted
  bright.

KING: And Ethiops of their sweet complexion crack.

DUMAIN: Dark needs no candles now, for dark is light.

BEROWNE: Your mistresses dare never come in rain,
  For fear their colours should be washed away.

KING: 'Twere good yours did: for sir to tell you plain,
  I'll find a fairer face not wash'd today.

BEROWNE: I'll prove her fair, or talk till Doomsday here.

KING: No devil will fright thee then so much as she.

DUMAIN: I never knew man hold vile stuff so dear.

LONGAVILLE: Look, here's thy love, my foot and her
  face see.

BEROWNE: O if the streets were paved with thine eyes,
  Her feet were much too dainty for such tread.

DUMAIN: O vile, then as she goes what upward lies?
  The street should see as she walk'd overhead.

KING: But what of this, are we not all in love?

BEROWNE: O nothing so sure, and thereby all forsworn.

KING: Then leave this chat, and good Berowne now prove
  Our loving lawful, and our faith not torn.

DUMAIN: Ay marry there, some flattery for this evil.

LONGAVILLE: O some authority how to proceed,
  Some tricks, some quillets, how to cheat the devil.

DUMAIN: Some salve for perjury.

BEROWNE: O 'tis more than need.
  Have at you then affection's men at arms,
  Consider what you first did swear unto:
  To fast, to study, and to see no woman:
  Flat treason 'gainst the kingly state of youth.
  Say, Can you fast? your stomachs are too young:
  And abstinence engenders maladies.
  And where that you have vowed to study (Lords)

In that each of you have forsworn his book.
Can you still dream and pore, and thereon look?
For when would you, my Lord, or you, or you,
Have found the ground of study's excellence,
Without the beauty of a woman's face:
From women's eyes this doctrine I derive,
They are the ground, the books, the Academes,
From whence doth spring the true Promethean fire.
Why, universal plodding prisons up
The nimble spirits in the arteries,
As motion and long-during action tires
The sinewy vigour of the traveller.
Now for not looking on a woman's face,
You have in that forsworn the use of eyes;
And study too, the causer of your vow.
For where is any Author in the world,
Teaches such beauty as a woman's eye:
Learning is but an adjunct to our self,
And where we are, our Learning likewise is.
Then when ourselves we see in Ladies' eyes,
Do we not likewise see our learning there?
O we have made a vow to study, Lords,
And in that vow we have forsworn our books:
For when would you (my Liege) or you, or you,
In leaden contemplation have found out
Such fiery numbers as the prompting eyes,
Of beauty's tutors have enrich'd you with?
Other slow Arts entirely keep the brain:
And therefore finding barren practisers,
Scarce show a harvest of their heavy toil.
But Love first learned in a Lady's eyes,
Lives not alone immured in the brain:
But with the motion of all elements,

Courses as swift as thought in every power,
And gives to every power a double power,
Above their functions and their offices.
It adds a precious seeing to the eye:
A Lover's eyes will gaze an eagle blind.
A Lover's ear will hear the lowest sound.
When the suspicious head of theft is stopp'd.
Love's feeling is more soft and sensible,
Than are the tender horns of cockled snails.
Love's tongue proves dainty, Bacchus gross in taste,
For valour, is not Love a Hercules?
Still climbing trees in the Hesperides.
Subtle as Sphinx, as sweet and musical,
As bright Apollo's lute, strung with his hair.
And when Love speaks, the voice of all the Gods,
Make heaven drowsy with the harmony.
Never durst Poet touch a pen to write,
Until his ink were tempered with Love's sighs:
O then his lines would ravish savage ears,
And plant in Tyrants mild humility.
From women's eyes this doctrine I derive.
They sparkle still the right Promethean fire,
They are the books, the Arts, the Academes,
That show, contain, and nourish all the world.
Else none at all in aught proves excellent.
Then fools you were these women to forswear,
Or keeping what is sworn, you will prove fools:
For Wisdom's sake, a word that all men love:
Or for Love's sake, a word that loves all men;
Or for men's sake, the author of these women:
Or women's sake, by whom we men are men.
Let us once lose our oaths to find ourselves,
Or else we lose ourselves, to keep our oaths:

It is religion to be thus forsworn.
For Charity itself fulfils the Law:
And who can sever love from Charity.
KING: Saint Cupid then, and soldiers to the field.
BEROWNE: Advance your standards, and upon them
Lords.
Pell-mell, down with them: but be first advis'd,
In conflict that you get the Sun of them.
LONGAVILLE: Now to plain dealing, Lay these glozes by,
Shall we resolve to woo these girls of France?
KING: And win them too, therefore let us devise,
Some entertainment for them in their tents.
BEROWNE: First from the park let us conduct them thither,
Then homeward every man attach the hand
Of his fair Mistress, in the afternoon
We will with some strange pastime solace them:
Such as the shortness of the time can shape,
For Revels, Dances, Masques, and merry hours,
Forerun fair Love, strewing her way with flowers.
KING: Away, away, no time shall be omitted
That will betime, and may by us be fitted.
BEROWNE: Alone, alone sowed cockle, reap'd no corn,
And Justice always whirls in equal measure:
Light wenches may prove plagues to men forsworn,
If so, our copper buys no better treasure.

Exeunt.

V. I

Enter Pedant, Curate, and Dull.

PEDANT: *Satis quod sufficit.*
CURATE: I praise God for you sir, your reasons at dinner
have been sharp and sententious: pleasant without scur-

rility, witty without affection, audacious without impudency, learned without opinion, and strange without heresy: I did converse this *quondam* day with a companion of the King's, who is intituled, nominated, or called Don Adriano de Armado.

PEDANT: *Novi hominem tanquam te,* His humour is lofty, his discourse peremptory: his tongue filed, his eye ambitious, his gait majestical, and his general behaviour vain, ridiculous, and thrasonical. He is too picked, too spruce, too affected, too odd, as it were, too peregrinate, as I may call it.

CURATE: A most singular and choice epithet.

Draw out his table-book.

PEDANT: He draweth out the thread of his verbosity, finer than the staple of his argument. I abhor such fanatical phantasims, such insociable and point device companions, such rackers of orthography, as to speak dout fine, when he should say doubt; det, when he should pronounce debt; d e b t, not det: he clepeth a calf, cauf: half, hauf; neighbour *vocatur* nebour; neigh abbreviated ne: this is abhominable, which he would call abbominable: It insinuateth me of insanie: *ne intelligis domine,* to make frantic, lunatic.

CURATE: *Laus deo, bene intelligo.*

PEDANT: *Bon, bon, fort bon.* Priscian, a little scratch'd, 'twill serve.

Enter Braggart, Boy, and Clown.

CURATE: *Videsne quis venit?*

PEDANT: *Video, et gaudeo.*

BRAGGART: Chirrah.

PEDANT: *Quare* chirrah, not sirrah?

BRAGGART: Men of peace well encounter'd.

PEDANT: Most military sir salutation.

BOY: They have been at a great feast of Languages, and stolen the scraps.

CLOWN: O they have liv'd long on the alms-basket of words. I marvel thy Master hath not eaten thee for a word, for thou art not so long by the head as *honorifica-bilitudinitatibus*: Thou art easier swallowed than a flap-dragon.

BOY: Peace, the peal begins.

BRAGGART: Mounsier, are you not letter'd?

BOY: Yes, yes, he teaches boys the horn-book: What is Ab spelt backward with the horn on his head?

PEDANT: Ba, *pueritia* with a horn added.

BOY: Ba most seely sheep, with a horn: you hear his learning.

PEDANT: *Quis quis*, thou consonant?

BOY: The third of the five vowels if you repeat them, or the fifth if I.

PEDANT: I will repeat them: a e i.

BOY: The sheep, the other two concludes it o u.

BRAGGART: Now by the salt wave of the Mediterraneum, a sweet touch, a quick venue of wit, snip snap, quick and home, it rejoiceth my intellect, true wit.

BOY: Offer'd by a child to an old man: which is wit-old.

PEDANT: What is the figure? What is the figure?

BOY: Horns.

PEDANT: Thou disputest like an infant: go whip thy gig.

BOY: Lend me your horn to make one, and I will whip about your infamy *circum circa* a gig of a cuckold's horn.

CLOWN: And I had but one penny in the world, thou shouldst have it to buy gingerbread: Hold, there is the very remuneration I had of thy Master, thou half-penny purse of wit, thou pigeon-egg of discretion. O and the heavens were so pleased, that thou wert but my bastard: What a joyful father wouldst thou make me? Go to, thou hast it *ad dungil*, at the finger's ends, as they say.

PEDANT: Oh I smell false Latin, *dunghel* for *unguem*.

BRAGGART: Artsman *preambulat,* we will be singled from the barbarous. Do you not educate youth at the Charge-house on the top of the Mountain?

PEDANT: Or *Mons* the hill.

BRAGGART: At your sweet pleasure, for the Mountain.

PEDANT: I do *sans question*.

BRAGGART: Sir, it is the King's most sweet pleasure and affection, to congratulate the Princess at her Pavilion, in the *posteriors* of this day, which the rude multitude call the afternoon.

PEDANT: The *posterior* of the day, most generous sir, is liable, congruent, and measurable for the afternoon: the word is well cull'd, chose, sweet, and apt I do assure you sir, I do assure.

BRAGGART: Sir, the King is a noble Gentleman, and my familiar, I do assure ye very good friend: for what is inward between us, let it pass. I do beseech thee remember thy courtesy. I beseech thee apparel thy head: and among other importunate and most serious designs, and of great import indeed too: but let that pass, for I must tell thee it will please his Grace (by the world) sometime to lean upon my poor shoulder, and with his royal finger thus dally with my excrement, with my mustachio: but sweet heart let that pass. By the world I recount no fable, some certain special honours it pleaseth his greatness to impart to Armado a soldier, a man of travel, that hath seen the world: but let that pass; the very all of all is: but sweet heart, I do implore

secrecy, that the King would have me present the
Princess (sweet chuck) with some delightful ostentation,
or show, or pageant, or antick, or firework: Now,
understanding that the Curate and your sweet self are
good at such eruptions, and sudden breaking out of
mirth (as it were) I have acquainted you withal, to the
end to crave your assistance.

PEDANT: Sir, you shall present before her the Nine
Worthies. Sir Nathaniel, as concerning some entertainment of time, some show in the posterior of this day, to
be rendered by our assistants at the King's command:
and this most gallant, illustrate and learned Gentleman,
before the Princess: I say none so fit as to present the
Nine Worthies.

CURATE: Where will you find men worthy enough to
present them?

PEDANT: Joshua, your self: my self, and this gallant gentleman, Judas Maccabaeus; this swain (because of his
great limb or joint) shall pass Pompey the Great, the
page Hercules.

BRAGGART: Pardon sir, error: He is not quantity enough
for that Worthy's thumb, he is not so big as the end of his
club.

PEDANT: Shall I have audience? he shall present Hercules
in minority: his *enter* and *exit* shall be strangling a snake;
and I will have an Apology for that purpose.

BOY: An excellent device: so if any of the audience hiss,
you may cry, Well done Hercules, now thou crushest
the snake; that is the way to make an offence gracious,
though few have the grace to do it.

BRAGGART: For the rest of the Worthies?

PEDANT: I will play three my self.

BOY: Thrice worthy Gentleman.

BRAGGART: Shall I tell you a thing?

PEDANT: We attend.

BRAGGART: We will have, if this fadge not, an Antique. I beseech you follow.

PEDANT: *Via* good-man Dull, thou hast spoken no word all this while.

CONSTABLE: Nor understood none neither sir.

PEDANT: Alone, we will employ thee.

CONSTABLE: I'll make one in a dance, or so: or I will play on the tabor to the Worthies, and let them dance the hay.

PEDANT: Most Dull, honest Dull, to our sport away.

Exeunt.

V.2

Enter Ladies.

PRINCESS: Sweet hearts we shall be rich ere we depart,
If fairings come thus plentifully in.
A Lady wall'd about with diamonds: Look you, what I
have from the loving King.

ROSALINE: Madam, came nothing else along with that?

PRINCESS: Nothing but this: yes as much love in rhyme,
As would be cramm'd up in a sheet of paper
Writ on both sides the leaf, margent and all,
That he was fain to seal on Cupid's name.

ROSALINE: That was the way to make his godhead wax:
For he hath been five thousand years a Boy.

KATHARINE: Ay, and a shrewd unhappy gallows too.

ROSALINE: You'll ne'er be friends with him, a' kill'd your sister.

KATHARINE: He made her melancholy, sad, and heavy,
And so she died: had she been light, like you,

Of such a merry nimble stirring spirit,
She might a' been a grandam ere she died.
And so may you: For a light heart lives long.

ROSALINE: What's your dark meaning mouse, of this
light word?

KATHARINE: A light condition in a beauty dark.

ROSALINE: We need more light to find your meaning out.

KATHARINE: You'll mar the light by taking it in snuff:
Therefore I'll darkly end the argument.

ROSALINE: Look what you do, you do it still i' th' dark.

KATHARINE: So do not you, for you are a light wench.

ROSALINE: Indeed I weigh not you, and therefore light.

KATHARINE: You weigh me not, O that's you care not
for me.

ROSALINE: Great reason: for past care, is still past cure.

PRINCESS: Well bandied both, a set of wit well played.
But Rosaline, you have a favour too?
Who sent it? And what is it?

ROSALINE: I would you knew.
And if my face were but as fair as yours,
My favour were as great, be witness this.
Nay, I have verses too, I thank Berowne,
The numbers true, and were the numb'ring too,
I were the fairest goddess on the ground.
I am compar'd to twenty thousand fairs.
O he hath drawn my picture in his letter.

PRINCESS: Any thing like?

ROSALINE: Much in the letters, nothing in the praise.

PRINCESS: Beauteous as ink: a good conclusion.

KATHARINE: Fair as a text B, in a copy book.

ROSALINE: 'Ware pencils. How? Let me not die your
debtor,
My red dominical, my golden letter.

O that your face were not so full of O's.

KATHARINE: A pox of that jest, and I beshrew all shrows:

PRINCESS: But Katharine, what was sent to you
From fair Dumain?

KATHARINE: Madam, this glove.

PRINCESS: Did he not send you twain?

KATHARINE: Yes Madam: and moreover,
Some thousand verses of a faithful Lover.
A huge translation of hypocrisy,
Vilely compiled, profound simplicity.

MARIA: This, and these pearls, to me sent Longaville.
The letter is too long by half a mile.

PRINCESS: I think no less: Dost thou not wish in heart
The chain were longer, and the letter short?

MARIA: Ay, or I would these hands might never part.

PRINCESS: We are wise girls to mock our Lovers so.

ROSALINE: They are worse fools to purchase mocking so.
That same Berowne I'll torture ere I go.
O that I knew he were but in by th' week,
How I would make him fawn, and beg, and seek,
And wait the season, and observe the times,
And spend his prodigal wits in bootless rhymes.
And shape his service wholly to my hests,
And make him proud to make me proud that jests.
So pertaunt like would I o'ersway his state,
That he should be my fool, and I his fate.

PRINCESS: None are so surely caught, when they are
catch'd,
As Wit turn'd fool, folly in wisdom hatch'd:
Hath wisdom's warrant, and the help of School,
And Wit's own grace to grace a learned Fool?

ROSALINE: The blood of youth burns not with such
excess,

As gravity's revolt to wantons be.

MARIA: Folly in Fools bears not so strong a note,
As fool'ry in the wise, when Wit doth dote:
Since all the power thereof it doth apply,
To prove by Wit, worth in simplicity.

Enter Boyet.

PRINCESS: Here comes Boyet, and mirth in his face.

BOYET: O I am stabb'd with laughter, Where's Her Grace?

PRINCESS: Thy news Boyet?

BOYET: Prepare Madam, prepare.
Arm Wenches arm, encounters mounted are,
Against your peace, Love doth approach, disguis'd:
Armed in arguments; you'll be surpris'd.
Muster your wits, stand in your own defence,
Or hide your heads like cowards, and fly hence.

PRINCESS: Saint Denis to Saint Cupid: What are they,
That charge their breath against us? Say scout say.

BOYET: Under the cool shade of a sycamore,
I thought to close mine eyes some half an hour:
When lo to interrupt my purpos'd rest,
Toward that shade I might behold address'd
The King and his companions: warily
I stole into a neighbour thicket by,
And overheard, what you shall overhear:
That by and by disguis'd they will be here.
Their Herald is a pretty knavish Page:
That well by heart hath conn'd his embassage,
Action and accent did they teach him there.
Thus must thou speak, and thus thy body bear.
And ever and anon they made a doubt,
Presence majestical would put him out:
For quoth the King, an Angel shalt thou see:
Yet fear not thou, but speak audaciously.

The Boy repli'd, An Angel is not evil,
I should have fear'd her had she been a devil.
With that all laugh'd, and clapp'd him on the shoulder,
Making the bold wag by their praises bolder.
One rubb'd his elbow thus, and fleer'd, and swore,
A better speech was never spoke before.
Another with his finger and his thumb,
Cried, *via*, we will do't come what will come.
The third he caper'd and cried, All goes well.
The fourth turn'd on the toe, and down he fell:
With that they all did tumble on the ground,
With such a zealous laughter so profound,
That in this spleen ridiculous appears,
To check their folly passion's solemn tears.

PRINCESS: But what, but what, come they to visit us?

BOYET: They do, they do; and are apparell'd thus,
Like Muscovites, or Russians, as I guess.
Their purpose is to parley, to court, and dance,
And everyone his love-feat will advance,
Unto his several Mistress: which they'll know
By favours several, which they did bestow.

PRINCESS: And will they so? the Gallants shall be task'd:
For Ladies, we will every one be mask'd,
And not a man of them shall have the grace
Despite of suit, to see a Lady's face.
Hold Rosaline, this favour thou shalt wear,
And then the King will court thee for his dear:
Hold, take thou this my sweet, and give me thine,
So shall Berowne take me for Rosaline.
And change your favours too, so shall your Loves
Woo contrary, deceiv'd by these removes.

ROSALINE: Come on then, wear the favours most in sight.

KATHARINE: But in this changing, what is your intent?

PRINCESS: The effect of my intent is to cross theirs:
  They do it but in mocking merriment,
  And mock for mock is only my intent.
  Their several counsels they unbosom shall,
  To Loves mistook, and so be mock'd withal,
  Upon the next occasion that we meet,
  With visages display'd to talk and greet.
ROSALINE: But shall we dance, if they desire us to 't?
PRINCESS: No, to the death we will not move a foot,
  Nor to their penn'd speech render we no grace:
  But while 'tis spoke, each turn away her face.
BOYET: Why that contempt will kill the keeper's heart,
  And quite divorce his memory from his part.
PRINCESS: Therefore I do it, and I make no doubt,
  The rest will ne'er come in, if he be out.
  There's no such sport, as sport by sport o'erthrown:
  To make theirs ours, and ours none but our own.
  So shall we stay mocking intended game,
  And they well mock'd, depart away with shame.
                    Sound.
BOYET: The trumpet sounds, be mask'd, the maskers come.
              The Ladies mask.
    Enter Blackamoors with music, the Boy with a speech,
          and the rest of the Lords disguised.
BOY: *All hail, the richest Beauties on the earth.*
BEROWNE: Beauties no richer than rich taffeta.
BOY: *A holy parcel of the fairest dames*
  That ever turn'd their backs to mortal views.
            The Ladies turn their backs to him.
BEROWNE: Their eyes villain, their eyes.
BOY: *That ever turn'd their eyes to mortal views.*
  Out —
BOYET: True, out indeed.

BOY: *Out of your favours heavenly spirits vouchsafe*
Not to behold.

BEROWNE: Once to behold, rogue.

BOY: *Once to behold with your Sun beamed eyes,*
With your Sun beamed eyes.

BOYET: They will not answer to that epithet.
You were best call it daughter beamed eyes.

BOY: They do not mark me, and that brings me out.

BEROWNE: Is this your perfectness? be gone you rogue.
Exit Boy.

ROSALINE: What would these strangers?
Know their minds Boyet.
If they do speak our language, 'tis our will
That some plain man recount their purposes.
Know what they would.

BOYET: What would you with the Princess?

BEROWNE: Nothing but peace, and gentle visitation.

ROSALINE: What would they, say they?

BOYET: Nothing but peace, and gentle visitation.

ROSALINE: Why that they have, and bid them so be gone.

BOYET: She says you have it, and you may be gone.

KING: Say to her we have measur'd many miles,
To tread a measure with you on this grass.

BOYET: They say that they have measur'd many a mile,
To tread a measure with you on this grass.

ROSALINE: It is not so. Ask them how many inches
Is in one mile? If they have measur'd many,
The measure then of one is easily told.

BOYET: If to come hither, you have measur'd miles,
And many miles: the Princess bids you tell,
How many inches doth fill up one mile?

BEROWNE: Tell her we measure them by weary steps.

BOYET: She hears herself.

ROSALINE: How many weary steps,
   Of many weary miles you have o'ergone,
   Are number'd in the travel of one mile?
BEROWNE: We number nothing that we spend for you,
   Our duty is so rich, so infinite,
   That we may do it still without accompt.
   Vouchsafe to show the sunshine of your face,
   That we (like savages) may worship it.
ROSALINE: My face is but a Moon, and clouded too.
KING: Blessed are clouds, to do as such clouds do.
   Vouchsafe bright Moon, and these thy stars to shine,
   (Those clouds removed) upon our watery eyne.
ROSALINE: O vain petitioner, beg a greater matter,
   Thou now request'st but moonshine in the water.
KING: Then in our measure, vouchsafe but one change.
   Thou bid'st me beg, this begging is not strange.
ROSALINE: Play music then: nay you must do it soon.
   Not yet no dance: thus change I like the Moon.
KING: Will you not dance? How come you thus estranged?
ROSALINE: You took the Moon at full, but now she's changed.
KING: Yet still she is the Moon, and I the Man.
   The music plays, vouchsafe some motion to it.
ROSALINE: Our ears vouchsafe it.
KING: But your legs should do it.
ROSALINE: Since you are strangers, and come here by chance,
   We'll not be nice, take hands, we will not dance.
KING: Why take we hands then?
ROSALINE: Only to part friends.
   Curtsy sweet hearts, and so the measure ends.
KING: More measure of this measure, be not nice.

ROSALINE: We can afford no more at such a price.

KING: Prize you yourself: What buys your company?

ROSALINE: Your absence only.

KING: That can never be.

ROSALINE: Then cannot we be bought: and so adieu,
Twice to your vizor, and half once to you.

KING: If you deny to dance, let's hold more chat.

ROSALINE: In private then.

KING: I am best pleas'd with that.

BEROWNE: White handed Mistress, one sweet word with
thee.

PRINCESS: Honey, and milk, and sugar: there is three.

BEROWNE: Nay then two treys, an if you grow so nice
Metheglin, wort, and malmsey; well run dice:
There's half a dozen sweets.

PRINCESS: Seventh sweet adieu, since you can cog,
I'll play no more with you.

BEROWNE: One word in secret.

PRINCESS: Let it not be sweet.

BEROWNE: Thou griev'st my gall.

PRINCESS: Gall, bitter.

BEROWNE: Therefore meet.

DUMAIN: Will you vouchsafe with me to change a word?

MARIA: Name it.

DUMAIN: Fair Lady.

MARIA: Say you so? Fair Lord:
Take that for your fair Lady.

DUMAIN: Please it you,
As much in private, and I'll bid adieu.

KATHARINE: What, was your vizard made without a
tongue?

LONGAVILLE: I know the reason Lady why you ask.

KATHARINE: O for your reason, quickly sir, I long.

LONGAVILLE: You have a double tongue within your mask,

And would afford my speechless vizard half.

KATHARINE: Veal quoth the Dutchman: is not veal a calf?

LONGAVILLE: A calf fair Lady?

KATHARINE: No, a fair Lord Calf.

LONGAVILLE: Let's part the word.

KATHARINE: No, I'll not be your half:

Take all and wean it, it may prove an ox.

LONGAVILLE: Look how you butt yourself in these sharp mocks.

Will you give horns chaste Lady? Do not so.

KATHARINE: Then die a calf before your horns do grow.

LONGAVILLE: One word in private with you ere I die.

KATHARINE: Bleat softly then, the butcher hears you cry.

BOYET: The tongues of mocking wenches are as keen

As is the razor's edge, invisible:

Cutting a smaller hair than may be seen,

Above the sense of sense so sensible:

Seemeth their conference, their conceits have wings,

Fleeter than arrows, bullets, wind, thought, swifter things.

ROSALINE: Not one word more my maids, break off, break off.

BEROWNE: By heaven, all dry-beaten with pure scoff.

KING: Farewell mad wenches, you have simple wits.

Exeunt King, Lords, and Blackamoors.

PRINCESS: Twenty adieus my frozen Muscovits.

Are these the breeds of wits so wondered at?

BOYET: Tapers they are, with your sweet breaths puff'd out.

ROSALINE: Well-liking wits they have, gross, gross, fat, fat.

PRINCESS: O poverty in wit, kingly poor flout.

Will they not (think you) hang themselves tonight?

Or ever but in vizards show their faces:
This pert Berowne was out of count'nance quite.
ROSALINE: They were all in lamentable cases.
The King was weeping ripe for a good word.
PRINCESS: Berowne did swear himself out of all suit.
MARIA: Dumain was at my service, and his sword:
No point (quoth I:) my servant straight was mute.
KATHARINE: Lord Longaville said I came o'er his heart:
And trow you what he call'd me?
PRINCESS: Qualm perhaps.
KATHARINE: Yes in good faith.
PRINCESS: Go sickness as thou art.
ROSALINE: Well, better wits have worn plain statute caps,
But will you hear; the King is my love sworn.
PRINCESS: And quick Berowne hath plighted faith to me.
KATHARINE: And Longaville was for my service born.
MARIA: Dumain is mine, as sure as bark on tree.
BOYET: Madam, and pretty mistresses give ear,
Immediately they will again be here
In their own shape: for it can never be,
They will digest this harsh indignity.
PRINCESS: Will they return?
BOYET: They will they will, God knows,
And leap for joy, though they are lame with blows:
Therefore change favours, and when they repair,
Blow like sweet roses, in this summer air.
PRINCESS: How blow? how blow? Speak to be under-
stood.
BOYET: Fair Ladies mask'd, are roses in their bud:
Dismask'd, their damask sweet commixture shown,
Are angels vailing clouds, or roses blown.
PRINCESS: Avaunt perplexity: What shall we do,
If they return in their own shapes to woo?

ROSALINE: Good Madam, if by me you'll be advis'd,
    Let's mock them still as well known as disguis'd.
    Let us complain to them what fools were here,
    Disguis'd like Muscovites in shapeless gear:
    And wonder what they were, and to what end
    Their shallow shows, and Prologue vilely penn'd,
    And their rough carriage so ridiculous,
    Should be presented at our tent to us.
BOYET: Ladies, withdraw: the gallants are at hand.
PRINCESS: Whip to our tents, as roes runs o'er land.
Exeunt.
Enter the King and the rest.
KING: Fair sir, God save you. Where's the Princess?
BOYET: Gone to her tent.
    Please it your Majesty command me any service to her?
KING: That she vouchsafe me audience for one word.
BOYET: I will, and so will she, I know my Lord.
Exit.
BEROWNE: This fellow pecks up wit as pigeons peas,
    And utters it again, when Jove doth please.
    He is Wit's peddler, and retails his wares,
    At Wakes, and Wassails, Meetings, Markets, Fairs.
    And we that sell by gross, the Lord doth know,
    Have not the grace to grace it with such show.
    This Gallant pins the wenches on his sleeve.
    Had he been Adam, he had tempted Eve.
    A' can carve too, and lisp: Why this is he,
    That kiss'd away his hand in courtesy.
    This is the Ape of Form, Monsieur the nice,
    That when he plays at Tables, chides the dice
    In honourable terms: Nay he can sing
    A mean most meanly, and in ushering
    Mend him who can: the Ladies call him sweet.

The stairs as he treads on them kiss his feet.
This is the flower that smiles on every one,
To show his teeth as white as whale's bone.
And consciences that will not die in debt,
Pay him the due of honey-tongued Boyet.

KING: A blister on his sweet tongue with my heart,
That put Armado's Page out of his part.

Enter the Ladies.

BEROWNE: See where it comes. Behaviour what wert thou,
Till this madman show'd thee? And what art thou now?

KING: All hail sweet Madam, and fair time of day.

PRINCESS: Fair in all Hail is foul, as I conceive.

KING: Construe my speeches better, if you may.

PRINCESS: Then wish me better, I will give you leave.

KING: We came to visit you, and purpose now
To lead you to our Court, vouchsafe it then.

PRINCESS: This field shall hold me, and so hold your vow:
Nor God, nor I, delights in perjur'd men.

KING: Rebuke me not for that which you provoke:
The virtue of your eye must break my oath.

PRINCESS: You nickname virtue: vice you should have
spoke:
For virtue's office never breaks men's troth.
Now by my maiden honour, yet as pure
As the unsallied lily, I protest,
A world of torments though I should endure,
I would not yield to be your house's guest:
So much I hate a breaking cause to be
Of heavenly oaths, vow'd with integrity.

KING: O you have liv'd in desolation here,
Unseen, unvisited, much to our shame.

PRINCESS: Not so my Lord, it is not so I swear,
We have had pastimes here, and pleasant game,

A mess of Russians left us but of late.

KING: How Madam? Russians?

PRINCESS: Ay in truth, my Lord.
Trim gallants, full of courtship and of state.

ROSALINE: Madam speak true. It is not so my Lord:
My Lady (to the manner of the days)
In courtesy gives undeserving praise.
We four indeed confronted were with four
In Russia habit: Here they stayed an hour,
And talk'd apace; and in that hour (my Lord)
They did not bless us with one happy word.
I dare not call them fools: but this I think,
When they are thirsty, fools would fain have drink.

BEROWNE: This jest is dry to me. Gentle sweet,
Your wit makes wise things foolish. When we greet
With eyes best seeing, heaven's fiery eye,
By light we lose light; your capacity
Is of that nature, that to your huge store,
Wise things seem foolish, and rich things but poor.

ROSALINE: This proves you wise and rich: for in my eye –

BEROWNE: I am a fool, and full of poverty.

ROSALINE: But that you take what doth to you belong,
It were a fault to snatch words from my tongue.

BEROWNE: O, I am yours, and all that I possess.

ROSALINE: All the fool mine.

BEROWNE: I cannot give you less.

ROSALINE: Which of the vizards was it that you wore?

BEROWNE: Where? When? What vizard?
Why demand you this?

ROSALINE: There, then, that vizard, that superfluous case,
That hid the worse, and show'd the better face.

KING: We are descried.
They'll mock us now downright.

DUMAIN: Let us confess, and turn it to a jest.

PRINCESS: Amaz'd my Lord? Why looks your Highness
    sad?

ROSALINE: Help hold his brows, he'll sound: why look
    you pale?

    Sea-sick I think coming from Muscovy.

BEROWNE: Thus pour the stars down plagues for perjury.

    Can any face of brass hold longer out?

    Here stand I, Lady dart thy skill at me,

    Bruise me with scorn, confound me with a flout.

    Thrust thy sharp wit quite through my ignorance.

    Cut me to pieces with thy keen conceit:

    And I will wish thee never more to dance,

    Nor never more in Russian habit wait.

    O! never will I trust to speeches penn'd,

    Nor to the motion of a schoolboy's tongue.

    Nor never come in vizard to my friend,

    Nor woo in rhyme like a blind harper's song,

    Taffeta phrases, silken terms precise,

    Three-pil'd hyperboles, spruce affectation;

    Figures pedantical, these summer flies,

    Have blown me full of maggot ostentation.

    I do forswear them, and I here protest,

    By this white glove (how white the hand God knows)

    Henceforth my wooing mind shall be express'd

    In russet yeas and honest kersey noes.

    And to begin Wench, so God help me law,

    My love to thee is sound, *sans* crack or flaw.

ROSALINE: *Sans sans,* I pray you.

BEROWNE: Yet I have a trick

    Of the old rage: bear with me, I am sick.

    I'll leave it by degrees: soft, let us see,

    Write *Lord have mercy on us,* on those three,

They are infected, in their hearts it lies:
They have the plague, and caught it of your eyes:
These Lords are visited, you are not free:
For the Lord's tokens on you do I see.

PRINCESS: No, they are free that gave these tokens to us.

BEROWNE: Our states are forfeit, seek not to undo us.

ROSALINE: It is not so; for how can this be true,
That you stand forfeit, being those that sue.

BEROWNE: Peace, for I will not have to do with you.

ROSALINE: Nor shall not, if I do as I intend.

BEROWNE: Speak for yourselves, my wit is at an end.

KING: Teach us sweet Madam, for our rude transgression,
some fair excuse.

PRINCESS: The fairest is confession.
Were not you here but even now, disguis'd?

KING: Madam, I was.

PRINCESS: And were you well advis'd?

KING: I was fair Madam.

PRINCESS: When you then were here,
What did you whisper in your Lady's ear?

KING: That more than all the world I did respect her.

PRINCESS: When she shall challenge this, you will reject
her.

KING: Upon mine honour no.

PRINCESS: Peace, peace, forbear:
Your oath once broke, you force not to forswear.

KING: Despise me when I break this oath of mine.

PRINCESS: I will, and therefore keep it. Rosaline,
What did the Russian whisper in your ear?

ROSALINE: Madam, he swore that he did hold me dear
As precious eyesight, and did value me
Above this World: adding thereto moreover,
That he would wed me, or else die my lover.

PRINCESS: God give thee joy of him: the noble Lord
Most honourably doth uphold his word.
KING: What mean you Madam?
By my life, my troth,
I never swore this Lady such an oath.
ROSALINE: By heaven you did; and to confirm it plain,
You gave me this: But take it sir again.
KING: My faith and this, the Princess I did give,
I knew her by this jewel on her sleeve.
PRINCESS: Pardon me sir, this jewel did she wear,
And Lord Berowne (I thank him) is my dear.
What? Will you have me, or your pearl again?
BEROWNE: Neither of either, I remit both twain.
I see the trick on't: Here was a consent,
Knowing aforehand of our merriment,
To dash it like a Christmas Comedy.
Some carry-tale, some please-man, some slight zany,
Some mumble-news, some trencher-knight, some Dick
That smiles his cheek in years, and knows the trick
To make my Lady laugh, when she's dispos'd;
Told our intents before: which once disclos'd,
The Ladies did change favours; and then we
Following the signs, woo'd but the sign of she.
Now to our perjury, to add more terror,
We are again forsworn in will and error.
Much upon this 'tis: and might not you
Forestall our sport, to make us thus untrue?
Do not you know my Lady's foot by th' squier?
And laugh upon the apple of her eye?
And stand between her back sir, and the fire,
Holding a trencher, jesting merrily?
You put our Page out: go, you are allow'd.
Die when you will, a smock shall be your shroud.

You leer upon me, do you? There's an eye
Wounds like a leaden sword.

BOYET: Full merrily hath this brave manage, this career,
been run.

BEROWNE: Lo, he is tilting straight. Peace, I have done.
Enter Clown.

Welcome pure wit, thou part'st a fair fray.

CLOWN: O Lord sir, they would know,
Whether the three Worthies shall come in, or no.

BEROWNE: What, are there but three?

CLOWN: No sir, but it is vara fine,
For every one pursents three.

BEROWNE: And three times thrice is nine.

CLOWN: Not so sir, under correction sir, I hope it is not so.
You cannot beg us sir, I can assure you sir, we know what
we know: I hope sir three times thrice sir.

BEROWNE: Is not nine.

CLOWN: Under correction sir, we know where–until it
doth amount.

BEROWNE: By Jove, I always took three threes for nine.

CLOWN: O Lord sir, it were pity you should get your
living by reckning sir.

BEROWNE: How much is it?

CLOWN: O Lord sir, the parties themselves, the actors sir
will show where–until it doth amount: for mine own
part, I am (as they say, but to perfect one man in one
poor man) Pompion the great sir.

BEROWNE: Art thou one of the Worthies?

CLOWN: It pleased them to think me worthy of Pompey
the Great: for mine own part, I know not the degree of
the Worthy, but I am to stand for him.

BEROWNE: Go, bid them prepare.

D

CLOWN: We will turn it finely off sir, we will take some care.
Exit.

KING: Berowne, they will shame us:
Let them not approach.

BEROWNE: We are shame-proof my Lord; and 'tis some
policy to have one show worse than the King's and his
company.

KING: I say they shall not come.

PRINCESS: Nay my good Lord, let me o'errule you now;
That sport best pleases, that doth least know how.
Where Zeal strives to content, and the contents
Dies in the zeal of that which it presents:
Their form confounded, makes most form in mirth,
When great things labouring perish in their birth.

BEROWNE: A right description of our sport my Lord.
Enter Braggart.

BRAGGART: Anointed, I implore so much expense of thy
royal sweet breath, as will utter a brace of words.

PRINCESS: Doth this man serve God?

BEROWNE: Why ask you?

PRINCESS: He speaks not like a man of God's making.

BRAGGART: That is all one my fair sweet honey Monarch:
For I protest, the Schoolmaster is exceeding fantastical:
Too too vain, too too vain. But we will put it (as they
say) to *fortuna de la guerra,* I wish you the peace of mind,
most royal couplement.
Exit.

KING: Here is like to be a good presence of Worthies;
He presents Hector of Troy, the Swain Pompey the
Great, the Parish Curate Alexander, Armado's page
Hercules, the Pedant Judas Maccabaeus: And if these
four Worthies in their first show thrive, these four will
change habits, and present the other five.

BEROWNE: There is five in the first show.

KING: You a.e deceived, 'tis not so.

BEROWNE: The Pedant, the Braggart, the Hedge Priest,
the Fool, and the Boy.

Abate throw at Novum, and the whole world again
Cannot pick out five such, take each one in's vein.

KING: The ship is under sail, and here she comes amain.

Enter Clown as Pompey.

CLOWN: *I Pompey am.*

BEROWNE: You lie, you are not he.

CLOWN: *I Pompey am.*

BOYET: With libbard's head on knee.

BEROWNE: Well said old mocker,
I must needs be friends with thee.

CLOWN: *I Pompey am, Pompey surnam'd the big.*

DUMAIN: The great.

CLOWN: It is great sir: *Pompey surnam'd the great:*
That oft in field, with targe and shield, did make my foe to
sweat:
And travelling along this coast, I here am come by chance,
And lay my arms before the legs of this sweet Lass of France.
If your Ladyship would say thanks Pompey, I had done.

PRINCESS: Great thanks great Pompey.

CLOWN: 'Tis not so much worth: but I hope I was perfect.
I made a little fault in great.

BEROWNE: My hat to a halfpenny, Pompey proves the best
Worthy.

Enter Curate for Alexander.

CURATE: *When in the world I liv'd, I was the world's*
Commander:
By East, West, North, and South, I spread my conquering
might
My scutcheon plain declares that I am Alisander.

BOYET: Your nose says no, you are not:
For it stands too right.

BEROWNE: Your nose smells no, in this most tender-
smelling Knight.

PRINCESS: The Conqueror is dismayed:
Proceed, good Alexander.

CURATE: *When in the world I lived, I was the world's Commander.*

BOYET: Most true, 'tis right: you were so Alisander.

BEROWNE: Pompey the great.

CLOWN: Your servant and Costard.

BEROWNE: Take away the Conqueror, take away Alisander.

CLOWN: O sir, you have overthrown Alisander the
conqueror: you will be scrap'd out of the painted cloth
for this: your Lion that holds his poleaxe sitting on a
close-stool, will be given to Ajax. He will be the ninth
Worthy. A Conqueror, and afraid to speak? Run away
for shame Alisander. There an't shall please you: a foolish
mild man, an honest man, look you, and soon dash'd.
He is a marvellous good neighbour in sooth, and a very
good Bowler: but for Alisander, alas you see, how 'tis a
little o'erparted. But there are Worthies a-coming, will
speak their mind in some other sort.

Exit Clown.

PRINCESS: Stand aside good Pompey.

Enter Pedant for Judas, and the Boy for Hercules.

PEDANT: Great Hercules is presented by this Imp,
Whose club kill'd Cerberus, that three-headed *canis*,
And when he was a babe, a child, a shrimp,
Thus did he strangle serpents in his *manus*;
Quoniam, he seemeth in minority,
Ergo, I come with this Apology.

Keep some state in thy *exit*, and vanish.

Exit Boy.

Judas I am.

DUMAIN: A Judas?

PEDANT: *Not Iscariot, sir.*

Judas I am, ycliped Maccabaeus.

DUMAIN: Judas Maccabaeus clipp'd, is plain Judas.

BEROWNE: A kissing traitor. How art thou prov'd Judas?

PEDANT: *Judas I am.*

DUMAIN: The more shame for you Judas.

PEDANT: What mean you sir?

BOYET: To make Judas hang himself.

PEDANT: Begin sir, you are my elder.

BEROWNE: Well follow'd, Judas was hang'd on an elder.

PEDANT: I will not be put out of countenance.

BEROWNE: Because thou hast no face.

PEDANT: What is this?

BOYET: A cittern head.

DUMAIN: The head of a bodkin.

BEROWNE: A death's face in a ring.

LONGAVILLE: The face of an old Roman coin, scarce seen.

BOYET: The pommel of Caesar's falchion.

DUMAIN: The carv'd-bone face on a flask.

BEROWNE: S. George's half cheek in a brooch.

DUMAIN: Ay, and in a brooch of lead.

BEROWNE: Ay, and worn in the cap of a tooth-drawer.
And now forward, for we have put thee in countenance.

PEDANT: You have put me out of countenance.

BEROWNE: False, we have given thee faces.

PEDANT: But you have out-fac'd them all.

BEROWNE: And thou wert a Lion, we would do so.

BOYET: Therefore as he is, an ass, let him go:
And so adieu sweet Jude. Nay, why dost thou stay?

DUMAIN: For the latter end of his name.

BEROWNE: For the *Ass* to the *Jude*, give it him. *Jud-as*, away.

PEDANT: This is not generous, not gentle, not humble.

BOYET: A light for Monsieur Judas, it grows dark, he may stumble.

PRINCESS: Alas poor Maccabaeus, how hath he been baited.

Enter Braggart.

BEROWNE: Hide thy head Achilles, here comes Hector in arms.

DUMAIN: Though my mocks come home by me, I will now be merry.

KING: Hector was but a Troyan in respect of this.

BOYET: But is this Hector?

KING: I think Hector was not so clean timber'd.

LONGAVILLE: His leg is too big for Hector's.

DUMAIN: More calf certain.

BOYET: No, he is best indued in the small.

BEROWNE: This cannot be Hector.

DUMAIN: He's a God or a Painter, for he makes faces.

BRAGGART: *The armipotent Mars, of lances the almighty,*
Gave Hector a gift.

DUMAIN: A gilt nutmeg.

BEROWNE: A lemon.

LONGAVILLE: Stuck with cloves.

DUMAIN: No cloven.

BRAGGART: *The armipotent Mars of lances the almighty,*
Gave Hector a gift, the heir of Ilion;
A man so breathed, that certain he would fight: yea
From morn till night, out of his Pavilion.
I am that flower.

DUMAIN: That mint.

LONGAVILLE: That columbine.

BRAGGART: Sweet Lord Longaville rein thy tongue.

LONGAVILLE: I must rather give it the rein: for it runs against Hector.

DUMAIN: Ay, and Hector's a greyhound.

BRAGGART: The sweet War-man is dead and rotten.
Sweet chucks, beat not the bones of the buried:
[But I will forward with my device;]
When he breathed, he was a man.
Sweet Royalty bestow on me the sense of hearing.

PRINCESS: Speak brave Hector, we are much delighted.

BRAGGART: I do adore thy sweet Grace's slipper.

BOYET: Loves her by the foot.

DUMAIN: He may not by the yard.

BRAGGART: *This Hector far surmounted Hannibal.*
The party is gone.

CLOWN: Fellow Hector, she is gone; she is two months on her way.

BRAGGART: What meanest thou?

CLOWN: Faith unless you play the honest Troyan, the poor wench is cast away: she's quick, the child brags in her belly already: 'tis yours.

BRAGGART: Dost thou infamonize me among Potentates? Thou shalt die.

CLOWN: Then shall Hector be whipp'd for Jaquenetta that is quick by him, and hang'd for Pompey, that is dead by him.

DUMAIN: Most rare Pompey.

BOYET: Renowned Pompey.

BEROWNE: Greater than great, great, great, great Pompey: Pompey the huge.

DUMAIN: Hector trembles.

BEROWNE: Pompey is moved, more Ates more Ates stir them, stir them on.

DUMAIN: Hector will challenge him.

BEROWNE: Ay, if a' have no more man's blood in's belly, than will sup a flea.

BRAGGART: By the North-pole I do challenge thee.

CLOWN: I will not fight with a pole like a Northern man; I'll slash, I'll do it by the sword: I pray you let me borrow my arms again.

DUMAIN: Room for the incensed Worthies.

CLOWN: I'll do it in my shirt.

DUMAIN: Most resolute Pompey.

PAGE: Master, let me take you a buttonhole lower: do you not see Pompey is uncasing for the combat: what mean you? you will lose your reputation.

BRAGGART: Gentlemen and Soldiers pardon me, I will not combat in my shirt.

DUMAIN: You may not deny it, Pompey hath made the challenge.

BRAGGART: Sweet bloods, I both may, and will.

BEROWNE: What reason have you for't?

BRAGGART: The naked truth of it is, I have no shirt, I go woolward for penance.

BOYET: True, and it was enjoined him in Rome for want of linen: since when, I'll be sworn he wore none, but a dishclout of Jaquenetta's, and he wears next his heart for a favour.

Enter a Messenger, Monsieur Marcade.

MARCADE: God save you Madam.

PRINCESS: Welcome Marcade, but that thou interrupt'st our merriment.

MARCADE: I am sorry Madam, for the news I bring is heavy in my tongue. The King your father –

PRINCESS: Dead for my life.

MARCADE: Even so: My tale is told.

BEROWNE: Worthies away, the Scene begins to cloud.

BRAGGART: For mine own part, I breathe free breath: I
have seen the day of wrong, through the little hole of
discretion, and I will right myself like a soldier.

Exeunt Worthies.

KING: How fares your Majesty?

PRINCESS: Boyet prepare, I will away tonight.

KING: Madam not so, I do beseech you stay.

PRINCESS: Prepare I say. I thank you gracious Lords
For all your fair endeavours and entreats:
Out of a new sad soul, that you vouchsafe,
In your rich wisdom to excuse, or hide,
The liberal opposition of our spirits,
If over-boldly we have borne ourselves,
In the converse of breath (your gentleness
Was guilty of it). Farewell worthy Lord:
A heavy heart bears not a nimble tongue.
Excuse me so, coming too short of thanks,
For my great suit, so easily obtain'd.

KING: The extreme parts of time, extremely forms
All causes to the purpose of his speed:
And often at his very loose decides
That, which long process could not arbitrate.
And though the mourning brow of progeny
Forbid the smiling courtesy of Love:
The holy suit which fain it would convince,
Yet since love's argument was first on foot,
Let not the cloud of sorrow justle it
From what it purpos'd; since to wail friends lost,
Is not by much so wholesome profitable,
As to rejoice at friends but newly found.

PRINCESS: I understand you not, my griefs are double.

BEROWNE: Honest plain words, best pierce the ear of grief

And by these badges understand the King.
For your fair sakes have we neglected time,
Play'd foul play with our oaths: your beauty Ladies
Hath much deformed us, fashioning our humours
Even to the opposed end of our intents.
And what in us hath seem'd ridiculous:
As Love is full of unbefitting strains,
All wanton as a child, skipping and vain.
Form'd by the eye, and therefore like the eye.
Full of strange shapes, of habits, and of forms
Varying in subjects as the eye doth roll,
To every varied object in his glance:
Which parti-coated presence of loose love
Put on by us, if, in your heavenly eyes,
Have misbecom'd our oaths and gravities,
Those heavenly eyes, that look into these faults,
Suggested us to make: therefore Ladies
Our love being yours, the error that Love makes
Is likewise yours. We to ourselves prove false,
By being once false, forever to be true
To those that make us both, fair Ladies you.
And even that falsehood in itself a sin,
Thus purifies itself, and turns to grace.

PRINCESS: We have receiv'd your letters, full of Love:
Your favours, the Ambassadors of Love.
And in our maiden council rated them,
At courtship, pleasant jest, and courtesy,
As bombast and as lining to the time:
But more devout than this in our respects
Have we not been, and therefore met your loves
In their own fashion, like a merriment.

DUMAIN: Our letters Madam, showed much more than jest.

LONGAVILLE: So did our looks.

ROSALINE: We did not coat them so.

KING: Now at that latest minute of the hour,
   Grant us your loves.

PRINCESS: A time methinks, too short,
   To make a world-without-end bargain in;
   No, no my Lord, your Grace is perjur'd much,
   Full of dear guiltiness, and therefore this:
   If for my Love (as there is no such cause)
   You will do aught, this shall you do for me.
   Your oath I will not trust: but go with speed
   To some forlorn and naked Hermitage,
   Remote from all the pleasures of the world:
   There stay, until the twelve Celestial Signs
   Have brought about the annual reckoning.
   If this austere insociable life,
   Change not your offer made in heat of blood:
   If frosts, and fasts, hard lodging, and thin weeds
   Nip not the gaudy blossoms of your Love,
   But that it bear this trial, and last love:
   Then at the expiration of the year,
   Come challenge me, challenge me by these deserts,
   And by this virgin palm, now kissing thine,
   I will be thine: and till that instant shut
   My woeful self up in a mourning house,
   Raining the tears of lamentation,
   For the remembrance of my Father's death.
   If this thou do deny, let our hands part,
   Neither entitled in the other's heart.

KING: If this, or more than this, I would deny,
   To flatter up these powers of mine with rest,
   The sudden hand of death close up mine eye.
   Hence ever then, my heart is in thy breast.

BEROWNE: And what to me my Love? and what to me?

ROSALINE: You must be purged too, your sins are rack'd.
You are attaint with faults and perjury:
Therefore if you my favour mean to get,
A twelvemonth shall you spend, and never rest,
But seek the weary beds of people sick.

DUMAIN: But what to me my love? but what to me?

KATHARINE: A wife? a beard, fair health, and honesty,
With threefold love, I wish you all these three.

DUMAIN: O shall I say, I thank you gentle wife?

KATHARINE: Not so my Lord, a twelvemonth and a day,
I'll mark no words that smooth fac'd wooers say.
Come when the King doth to my Lady come:
Then if I have much love, I'll give you some.

DUMAIN: I'll serve thee true and faithfully till then.

KATHARINE: Yet swear not, lest ye be forsworn again.

LONGAVILLE: What says Maria?

MARIA: At the twelvemonth's end,
I'll change my black gown, for a faithful friend.

LONGAVILLE: I'll stay with patience: but the time is long.

MARIA: The liker you, few taller are so young.

BEROWNE: Studies my Lady? Mistress, look on me,
Behold the window of my heart, mine eye:
What humble suit attends thy answer there,
Impose some service on me for my love.

ROSALINE: Oft have I heard of you my Lord Berowne,
Before I saw you: and the world's large tongue
Proclaims you for a man replete with mocks,
Full of comparisons, and wounding flouts:
Which you on all estates will execute,
That lie within the mercy of your wit.
To weed this wormwood from your fruitful brain,
And therewithal to win me, if you please,

Without the which I am not to be won,
You shall this twelvemonth term from day to day,
Visit the speechless sick, and still converse
With groaning wretches: and your task shall be,
With all the fierce endeavour of your wit,
To enforce the pained impotent to smile.

BEROWNE: To move wild laughter in the throat of death?
It cannot be, it is impossible.
Mirth cannot move a soul in agony.

ROSALINE: Why that's the way to choke a gibing spirit,
Whose influence is begot of that loose grace,
Which shallow laughing hearers give to fools:
A jest's prosperity, lies in the ear
Of him that hears it, never in the tongue
Of him that makes it: then, if sickly ears,
Deaf'd with the clamours of their own dear groans,
Will hear your idle scorns, continue then,
And I will have you, and that fault withal.
But if they will not, throw away that spirit,
And I shall find you empty of that fault,
Right joyful of your reformation.

BEROWNE: A twelvemonth? Well: befall what will befall,
I'll jest a twelvemonth in an Hospital.

PRINCESS: Ay sweet my Lord, and so I take my leave.

KING: No Madam, we will bring you on your way.

BEROWNE: Our wooing doth not end like an old Play:
Jack hath not Jill: these Ladies' courtesy
Might well have made our sport a Comedy.

KING: Come sir, it wants a twelvemonth and a day,
And then 'twill end.

BEROWNE: That's too long for a play.

Enter Braggart.

BRAGGART: Sweet Majesty vouchsafe me.

PRINCESS: Was not that Hector?

DUMAIN: The worthy Knight of Troy.

BRAGGART: I will kiss thy royal finger, and take leave. I am a Votary, I have vow'd to Jaquenetta to hold the plough for her sweet love three years. But most esteemed greatness, will you hear the Dialogue that the two Learned men have compiled, in praise of the Owl and the Cuckoo? It should have followed in the end of our show.

KING: Call them forth quickly, we will do so.

BRAGGART: Holla, approach.

Enter all.

This side is Hiems, Winter.

This Ver, the Spring; the one maintained by the Owl,

T'other by the cuckoo.

Ver, begin.

The Song.
Spring.

When daisies pied, and violets blue,
And cuckoo-buds of yellow hue:
And lady-smocks all silver-white
Do paint the meadows with delight,
The cuckoo then on every tree,
Mocks married men, for thus sings he,
Cuckoo,
Cuckoo, cuckoo: O word of fear,
Unpleasing to a married ear.

When shepherds pipe on oaten straws,
And merry larks are ploughmen's clocks:
When turtles tread, and rooks and daws,
And maidens bleach their summer smocks:
The cuckoo then, on every tree
Mocks married men; for thus sings he,

Cuckoo.
Cuckoo, cuckoo: O word of fear,
Unpleasing to a married ear.

Winter.
When icicles hang by the wall,
And Dick the Shepherd blows his nail;
And Tom bears logs into the hall,
And milk comes frozen home in pail:
When blood is nipp'd, and ways be foul,
Then nightly sings the staring Owl
Tu-whit to-who.
 A merry note,
  While greasy Joan doth keel the pot.

When all aloud the wind doth blow,
And coughing drowns the Parson's saw:
And birds sit brooding in the snow,
And Marian's nose looks red and raw:
When roasted crabs hiss in the bowl,
Then nightly sings the staring Owl,
Tu-whit to-who:
 A merry note,
  While greasy Joan doth keel the pot.

BRAGGART: The words of Mercury,
 Are harsh after the songs of Apollo:
 You that way; we this way.
   Exeunt Omnes.

NOTES

References are to the page and line of this edition; there are 33 lines to the full page.

The Actors' Names. In the Folio Text there is con- P. 20 siderable inconsistency in the names of speakers; thus Ferdinand is sometimes 'King' and at others 'Duke'; the Princess of France occasionally is 'Queen'; Costard is usually 'Clown', Armado usually 'Braggart' etc. It seemed more in keeping with the style of the play to follow the Folio in preserving the type names of the comic characters – Clown, Braggart, Maid, Curate, Pedant and Boy (who is sometimes also Page).

Academe: i.e. like the famous Academy at Athens P. 21 L. 16 where Plato taught.

Still . . . art: always pondering over the art of living. P. 21 L. 17

common sense: normal perception. P. 23 L. 5

pain . . . pain: This play is full of words used with as P. 23 L. 14 many senses as possible.

Who dazzling so: i.e., by the dazzling beauty of his P. 23 L. 23 lady's eyes.

earthly . . . lights: i.e. astronomers who give names to P. 23 L. 29 the stars.

Proceeded: literally, taken a degree, shown himself a P. 24 L. 3 scholar.

weeds . . . weeding: he plucks out the corn and lets the P. 24 L. 4 weeds grow.

fashion's own Knight: It was the mark of an accom- P. 26 L. 29 plished gentleman to be able to converse in the latest fashion of vocabulary.

Duke: see Note on the Actor's Names above. P. 26 L. 33

P. 27 L. 2   *reprehend:* Constable Dull, like others of Shake-speare's humble characters, uses long words but is not always sure of their meanings.

P. 27 L. 9   *contempts:* for contents.

P. 27 L. 21   *with the manner:* in the act.

P. 28 L. 27   *curious-knotted:* elaborately laid out, with little hedges of box.

P. 29 L. 4   *continent canon:* law of continence.

P. 29 L. 5   *passion to say:* say with grief.

P. 30 L. 4   *serve your turn:* help.

P. 31 L. 7   *congruent epitheton:* appropriate epithet.

P. 31 L. 27   *crosses:* money – because the reverse of an Eliza-bethan coin was divided with a cross.

P. 32 L. 5   *deuce-ace:* a throw of dice showing two and one.

P. 32 L. 12   *dancing horse:* a famous performing horse called Morocco, owned by a man called Banks, which performed circus tricks.

P. 32 L. 20   *courtesy:* Court compliment.

P. 32 L. 28   *carried the town gates:* see Judges 16: 1–3.

P. 33 L. 2   *complexion:* i.e. of which of the four humours – sanguine, melancholy, choleric, or phlegmatic.

P. 33 L. 30   *King and the Beggar:* the story of King Cophetua who married a beggar girl.

P. 34 L. 6   *rational hind:* intelligent peasant.

P. 34 L. 17   *allowed . . . day-woman:* assigned to the dairy woman.

P. 35 L. 11   *fast and loose:* a cheating game.

P. 35 L. 29   *butt shaft:* arrow used for target practice.

P. 35 L. 31   *first and second cause:* technical reasons for a duel; this matter is acutely discussed by Touchstone in *As You Like It,* V. vi. 50–108.

P. 35 L. 32   *passado:* thrust. *duello:* rules of duelling.

P. 35 L. 33   *called boy:* a desperate insult.

P. 36 L. 5   *folio:* volumes of the largest size.

P. 38 L. 11   *Alençon:* spelt Alanson in the Folio.

P. 38 L. 19   *begets occasion:* finds opportunities.

conceit's expositor: witty commentator on wit.   P. 38 L. 22

this Court: i.e. the sky.   P. 39 L. 12

mask: Fashionable ladies wore masks to protect their   P. 40 L. 11
complexions from the sun and to preserve the pink
and white complexion which was regarded as the
sign of feminine beauty.

Fair fall: good luck to.   P. 40 L. 12

depart withal: part with.   P. 41 L. 1

arrest . . . word: formally take you at your word.   P. 41 L. 15

let it blood: bleeding was a remedy for many com-   P. 42 L. 11
plaints.

margent: margin. *coat:* quote, note. The notes in   P. 44 L. 18
learned books were usually printed in the margin.

dispos'd: i.e. to mirth.   P. 44 L. 22

father: i.e. Jupiter.   P. 44 L. 31

Concolinel: probably the title of the song which   P. 45 L. 11
Moth sings.

brawl: a French dance of the follow-my-leader kind.   P. 45 L. 15

hat penthouse-like: i.e. pulled down over the eyes –   P. 45 L. 23
the sign of a melancholy lover.

thinbelly doublet: close fitting jacket.   P. 45 L. 24

The hobbyhorse is forgot: a popular tune. The hobby-   P. 46 L. 3
horse was an imitation horse worn by certain
performers in a morris dance; the word also means
prostitute.

Costard: head – a slang word.   P. 47 L. 15

broken in a shin: with the skin of the shin broken.   P. 47 L. 15

l'envoy: explained later in lines.   P. 47 L. 17

salve in the mail: ointment in the bag.   P. 47 L. 18

plantan: a broad leafed weed regarded as good for   P. 47 L. 19
bruises.

The fox . . . : These lines are presumably a topical   P. 47 L. 31
jest at the expense of certain persons well known to
the original audience. In Queen Elizabeth's Court
great men were usually endowed with nicknames.

Thus Leicester was called the Bear, Burghley the Fox, and Robert Cecil was called the Elf.

P. 48 L. 5   *stayed the odds*: i.e. turned them into evens by adding up the total to four.

P 48 L. 14   *bargain*: bad bargain.

P. 50 L. 20   *counsel*: secret communication.

P. 50 L. 27   *beadle*: the parish officer who whipped offenders, such as prostitutes.

P. 51 L. 5   *paritors*: apparitors, officers of the Ecclesiastical Court, who summoned offenders guilty of offences against morality.

P. 51 L. 9   *clock*: the Folio reads *cloak*.

P. 51 L. 24   *Joan*: a country wench.

P. 52 L. 4   *stand ... in*: The Princess hunts after the manner of Queen Elizabeth. The Queen and her Ladies took up their stand and the deer were driven past them well within bowshot range.

P. 52 L. 16   *good my glass*: my good mirror.

P. 52 L. 20   *heresy in fair*: heresy against beauty.

P. 53 L. 25   *break up*: (a) carve a chicken and (b) open a letter.

P. 54 L. 24   *Nemean lion*: a fierce beast slain by Hercules.

P. 54 L. 30   *plume of feathers*: i.e. fantastical gallant.

P. 55 L. 2   *going ... erewhile*: if you have met it before.

P. 55 L. 6   *Monarcho*: a crazy Italian who haunted Queen Elizabeth's Court.

P. 55 L. 19   *shooter*: with a pun on suitor.

P. 55 L. 24   *horns ... miscarry*: i.e. if someone is not made a cuckold. Cuckolds were said to wear invisible horns.

P. 55 L. 25   *Finely put on*: well answered.

P. 55 L. 30   *strikes ... brow*: aims at your head.

P. 56 L. 2   *Pepin ... boy*: Pepin was the father of Charlemagne, and therefore lived a long while ago.

P. 56 L. 3   *hit it*: the name of a tune.

P. 56 L. 5   *Guinever*: King Arthur's Queen.

P. 56 L. 17   *Wide ... bow hand*: i.e. too far to the left.

pin: peg in the middle of the target.   P. 56 L. 21

rubbing: literally, unevenness on the bowling green.   P. 56 L. 25

Sola, sola: i.e. an imitation of the hunting horn.   P. 57 L. 5

IV. 2: In this scene the pedantic ways of the learned are parodied; contemporaries probably noted certain parallels with well known individuals which cannot now be identified.

first head: a buck with its antlers fully developed, i.e.   P. 57 L. 18
in the fifth year.

haud credo: I don't believe it.   P. 57 L. 19

Twice-sod: twice-boiled – which is also the meaning   P. 57 L. 30
of *bis coctus.*

patch set on learning: a fool set to learn.   P. 58 L. 12

Dictynna: a title of Phoebe or Diana, the moon.   P. 58 L. 20

affect the letter: indulge in alliteration.   P. 59 L. 8

put ell: i.e. add 50 (L in Roman numerals).   P. 59 L. 14

talent: with a pun on *talon.*   P. 59 L. 20

ventricle: that division of the brain which was sup-   P. 59 L. 26
posed to hold the memory.

vir ... loquitur: it's a wise man who speaks few words.   P. 60 L. 3

Fauste ... Ruminat: Faustus, I pray you when all   P. 60 L. 17
your flock lies feeding under the cool shade – opening
lines from the Eclogues of Baptista Spagnoli of
Mantua which were a textbook for schoolboys
in Shakespeare's day.

Venetia ... pretia: Who has not seen thee does not   P. 60 L. 21
prize thee – an Italian proverb.

Ut ... fa: Here he hums a scale.   P. 60 L. 24

bias: literally, the curved course of a bowl, so in-   P. 61 L. 3
clination.

Here ... caret: i.e. the verses do scan but the poetry is   P. 61 L. 16
wanting *(caret).*

stay not: don't wait to show your respect *(com-*   P. 62 L. 3
pliment).

colourable colours: plausible excuses.   P. 62 L. 11

IV.3 : This scene needs the stage for its effect. As each lover comes in and hides he is unaware of the others who have entered before him, and by stage convention is supposed not to hear their comments.

P. 63 L. 8   *mad as Ajax :* Ajax disappointed that the shield of the dead Achilles was not awarded to himself went mad and slew a flock of sheep supposing them to be his enemies.

P. 63 L. 25   *bird bolt :* blunt arrow used for shooting small birds.

P. 64 L. 18   *perjure :* Perjurors were compelled to stand in the pilllory wearing a paper declaring their offence.

P. 64 L. 26   *Tyburn :* the gallows at Tyburn was permanent and three-cornered.

P. 65 L. 17   *liver vein :* humour of a lover, the liver being regarded as the seat of love.

P. 65 L. 33   *Her amber . . . coted :* amber itself has noted (*coted*) that her hair is more amber than amber.

P. 66 L. 3   *with child :* i.e. burdened.

P. 68 L. 5   *coaches :* see p. 64 l. 4.

P. 68 L. 11   *moth . . . beam :* see Luke 6 : 41–42. *moth :* mote, speck of dust.

P. 68 L. 17   *gig :* spinning top, rotated by a whip.

P. 68 L. 19   *Nestor :* the oldest and gravest of the Greek generals at the siege of Troy.

P. 68 L. 24   *caudle :* hot drink, especially for those suffering from heartburn.

P. 70 L. 33   *cull'd sovereignty :* selected pre-eminence.

P. 71 L. 21   *School of night :* see Introduction, p. 17.

P. 71 L. 30   *native blood :* natural colour.

P. 72 L. 10   *devil . . . fright :* The devil was represented in pictures as black : devil was pronounced 'deal'.

P. 72 L. 27   *affection's men at arms :* Love's bodyguard.

P. 73 L. 8   *Promethean :* heavenly, for Prometheus stole the fire of the gods and gave it to men.

P. 73 L. 9   *prisons :* the Folio reads 'poisons'.

suspicious . . . stopp'd: A much discussed line; if the reading is correct, it means the hearing of a thief who is naturally suspicious of every sound. P. 74 L. 7

Hesperides: the garden where grew the Golden Apples which Hercules stole. P. 74 L. 12

get . . . them: come at them when the sun is in their eyes. P. 75 L. 8

Sowed . . . corn: i.e. if you sow weeds, you won't reap corn. P. 75 L. 22

Satis . . . sufficit: that which suffices is enough. P. 75 L. 29

Novi . . . te: I know the man as well as I know you. P. 76 L. 6

staple: literally, a fibre of wool. P. 76 L. 15

rackers of orthography: torturers of spelling. P. 76 L. 17

insinuateth . . . insanie: suggests insanity to me. P. 76 L. 22

Laus . . . intelligo: Praise be to God, I understand you well. P. 76 L. 24

Priscian . . . scratch'd: i.e. your Latin is not too good. Priscian was a famous Latin grammarian about whom there was a proverb 'to break Priscian's head' – to speak bad Latin. P. 76 L. 25

Videsne . . . gaudeo: do you see who comes? I see and rejoice. P. 76 L. 28

alms-basket: basket in which alms were collected for the poor. P. 77 L. 3

honorificabilitudinatibus: a scholar's joke, for it is the longest word in the Latin language, meaning 'in the condition of being loaded with honours.' P. 77 L. 5

flapdragon: a lighted raisin which was floated on liquor and had to be swallowed. P. 77 L. 6

horn-book: the first reading book; a single sheet, mounted on a wooden board with a handle, and covered with transparent horn. P. 77 L. 10

pueritia: childishness, 'my little one.' P. 77 L. 12

wit-old: with a pun on *wittol:* a complacent cuckold. P. 77 L. 23

circum circa: round and round, Theobald's emendation for *unum cita.* P. 77 L. 28

P. 77. L. 33   *pigeon-egg*: i.e. smooth little thing.

P. 77 L. 3   *ad dungil*: for *ad unguem* (at the finger nail) – a schoolboy's joke.

P. 78 L. 6   *Artsman preambulat*: scholar, go first.

P. 78 L. 8   *Charge-house . . . mountain*: another topical joke, now unintelligible. Presumably a *charge-house* is a school where fees are charged (contrasted with a free-school).

P. 78 L. 22   *remember . . . courtesy*: i.e. don't forget your manners – take off your hat in the presence of such an important person; but as a gesture of politeness Armado immediately asks him to put it on again.

P. 78 L. 28   *excrement*: anything growing out of the body, such as hair.

P. 79 L. 8   *Nine Worthies*: the Nine Famous Men of History, usually Hector of Troy, Alexander the Great, and Julius Caesar (from classical story): Joshua, King David, and Judas Maccabeus from the Bible; King Arthur, Charlemagne, and Geoffrey of Bouillon from European legend. Shakespeare, however, includes Pompey and Hercules.

P. 79 L. 25   *strangling a snake*: Hercules as an infant strangled two snakes, one in either hand, which attacked him in his cradle.

P. 80 L. 27   *shrewd . . . gallows*: cunning luckless rogue.

P. 80 L. 31   *light . . . light*: Another elaborate play on the various
P. 81 L. 32   meanings of *light* – light-hearted, trifling, frivolous, illumination, candlelight, wanton, lightweight. Compare p. 23 l. 13 – p. 24 l. 1.

P. 81 L. 8   *in snuff*: in anger, with a pun on the *snuff* (smoking wick) of a candle.

P. 81 L. 16   *bandied*: exchanged; literally, the exchange of strokes in tennis.

P. 81 L. 23   *numbers*: metrical feet. *numb'ring*: estimation.

P. 81 L. 23   *red dominical*: the red letters used to denote Sundays and Feast days in the almanack, with reference to Katharine's red hair. Red and gold were not always distinguished in Shakespeare's time.

O's: smallpox scars.   P. 82 L. I

pertaunt like: This is the reading in Quarto and P. 82 L. 25 Folio; it has been much emended. The word obviously means 'tyrannical'; the best guess is 'like Dame Partlet' – the domineering wife of Chanticleer.

favours several: particular gifts.   P. 84 L. 21

Despite of suit: in spite of their petitions.   P. 84 L. 25

tread a measure: dance. The measure was a stately P. 86 L. 23 dance used on formal occasions.

change: i.e., of time.   P. 87 L. 15

trey: throw of three at dice.   P. 88 L. 13

Veal . . . Dutchman: the Dutchman's pronunciation P. 89 L. 4 of 'well', with the inevitable pun on calf.

kingly poor: an execrable pun on well– li-king.   P. 89 L. 32

weeping ripe: on point of bursting into tears.   P. 90 L. 4

out . . . suit: out of court.   P. 90 L. 5

statute caps: flat woollen caps worn by citizens and P. 90 L. 13 apprentices.

Blow: open like rosebuds – i.e. take off your masks. P. 90 L. 26

damask sweet commixture: pink-and-white complex- P. 90 L. 30 ions.

Ape of Form: imitator of fashion.   P. 91 L. 29

whale's: pronounced as a two syllable word.   P. 92 L. 3

When . . . light: i.e. you are the sun which blinds by P. 93 L. 15 excessive light.

Three-pil'd: excessive; the word denotes velvet of the P. 94 L. 20 thickest quality.

russet . . . kersey: kinds of homespun cloth.   P. 94 L. 26

Lord . . . us: The warning words painted on the doors P. 94 L. 33 of houses infected with the plague. There had been a particularly bad outbreak in 1592–93.

Lord's tokens: signs of the plague, and also the gifts of P. 95 L. 4

the lovers which the Ladies are wearing.

P. 95 L. 26   *force not:* find no difficulty in.

P. 96 L. 19   *in years:* into wrinkles.

P. 96 L. 25   *in will and error:* deliberately and by mistake.

P. 96 L. 29   *laugh . . . eye:* jest intimately.

P. 96 L. 32   *allow'd:* i.e. a privileged fool.

P. 97 L. 15   *beg us:* claim us as fools – from the legal procedure in the Court of Wards whereby interested parties begged the Court for the custody of a minor or an idiot.

P. 98 L. 10   *that sport . . . birth:* i.e. the unrehearsed efforts of a too ambitious play are the most amusing.

P. 98 L. 15   *sport:* i.e. the fiasco of the Muscovite Masque.

P. 99 L. 3   *Hedge Priest:* illiterate lowgrade priest.

P. 99 L. 5   *Abate . . . Novum:* except for a throw of nine at novum – a dice game at which the principal throws were 5 and 9.

P. 99 L. 12   *libbard's head . . . knee:* The joke has not been explained but presumably Pompey bears as his device a leopard or leopard's head. Each of the Worthies carries a symbolic shield or device.

P. 100 L. 2   *too right:* Alexander the Great's head was slightly twisted; he was said also to have had a most sweet smelling skin.

P. 100 L. 15   *painted cloth:* imitation tapestry, painted with scenes from ancient legend or the Bible. Alexander's coat of arms was a lion sitting on a throne and holding a battleaxe. Ajax was noted among the Greeks for his boasting. After the publication (1596) of Sir John Harington's *Metamorphosis of Ajax* – a rabelaisian discourse on Harington's invention of a form of primitive water-closet – the name Ajax was inseparably connected with a privy.

P. 100 L. 23   *o'erparted:* not up to the part.

P. 101 L. 13   *my elder:* i.e. you seem to know more about it than I do.

cittern head: the top of a cittern (a form of guitar), P. 101 L. 18
often carved with a face.

have no shirt: – a confession of extreme and ungenteel P. 104 L. 20
poverty.

go woolward: wear wool next my skin. P. 104 L. 20

The extreme . . . speed: in extremity everything must P. 105 L. 20
be done speedily.

at . . . loose: at random. P. 105 L. 22

coat: (also spelt cote), quote, note. P. 107 L. 2

a beard: i.e. I wish you would grow up. P. 108 L. 8

wounding flouts: bitter jests which hurt. P. 108 L. 29

all estates: all kinds of men. P. 108 L. 30

jest's prosperity: the success of a jest. P. 109 L. 13

Ladies' courtesy: i.e. if these Ladies had been kind to P. 109 L. 27
us.

Comedy: Shakespeare's definition of a Comedy is P. 109 L. 28
thus 'a play which ends happily in wedding'.

Cuckoo . . . fear: The cry 'cuckoo' warned a cuckold P. 110 L. 25
that his wife's lover was at hand.

blows his nail: i.e. to keep warm. P. 111 L. 6

GLOSSARY

accompt : account.

acquittance : receipt.

address'd : ready, directed.

affection : affectation.

affects : natural qualities.

amazes : astonishes.

annothanize : dissect.

apostrophas : poetic omission of a vowel.

arm'd : resolute.

aspect : appearance.

Ates : goddesses of mischief.

attach : arrest.

attaint : charged.

attainder : condemnation.

badges : tokens.

bait'd : tormented.

barbarism : lack of book learning.

bate : blunt.

benvenuto : welcome.

beshrew : curse.

blown : blown out, swollen.

bombast : padding.

by : concerning.

canary : a dance.

canis : dog.

carnation : red.

catastrophe : conclusion.

carve : be affected.

chapmen : salesmen.

codpiece : opening in the hose.

cog : cheat.

common : commonplace.

competitors : companions.

complements : fine behaviour, accompaniments.

conceits : witticisms.

condign : deserved.

conn'd : learnt by heart.

construe : translate.

cormorant : a rapacious bird.

convince : win.

counsels : secret thoughts.

couplement : pair.

courtesy : sign of respect towards.

crab : crab apple.

cross : thwart.

curst : shrewish.

dash : make fun of.

dear : good, valuable.

debate : strife.

descried : found out.

degree : rank.

dig-you-den : good evening to you.

dominator : ruler.

dry-beaten : beaten without

breaking the skin.

enfranchize : liberate.
entitled : having legal claim to.
epilogues : conclusions.
ergo : therefore.
eunuch : guardian of a harem.
eyen : eyes.

fadge : be suitable.
fairings : presents.
fame : report.
familiar : attendant spirit.
favour : (1) love token (2) complexion.
festinately : hastily.
filed : polished.
fleer'd : grinned contemptuously.
flout : jest.

gear : stuff.
generous : well born, noble.
glaz'd : enclosed in glass.
glozes : excuses.
grace : beauty, charm, favour.
green : immature.
green geese : goslings.
guerdon : reward.

hackney : horse available for common hire.
half cheek : profile.
hay : a country dance.
hests : commands.
hight : named.

housekeeping : hospitality.
humours : whims.
humorously : melancholy.

incony : fine.
infamonize : disgrace.
infants : buds.
ingenuous : quick-witted.
inkle : piece of tape.
intellect : purport.
interim : pastime.
it : its.

Juvenal : juvenile, youth.

keel : cool.
keep : dwell.

leaden : blunt.
liable : appropriate.
Liege : lord.
love-feast : act of courting.

manage : display of horsemanship.
manus : hand.
margent : margin.
mean : tenor.
meed : reward.
mess : party of four.
mete : aim.
metheglim : mead (drink made of honey).
minime : not in the least.
mounted : prepared.

nice : dainty.

nickname : give a wrong name to.

omne bene : all well.

opinion : arrogance.

overshot : wide of the mark.

painful : laborious.

painted : artificial.

part : divide.

pass : play the part of.

pavilion : tent.

pen : penmanship.

peregrinate : foreign.

perge : proceed.

phantisime : fantastic.

pia mater : brain.

placket : opening in the petticoat.

please-man : yes-man.

point-device : precise.

policy : wisdom.

pomewater : a juicy kind of apple.

Pompion : pumpkin.

prick : centre of the target.

pricket : buck of the first year.

pruning : preening.

quare : why.

quis : who.

quondam : former.

quoniam : since.

rack'd : tortured.

rage : poetic fury.

reek : steam.

removes : changes.

repair : come again.

repasture : food.

sable-coloured : black.

saw : wise saying, platitude.

scutcheon : heraldic shield.

sensibly : feelingly.

several : (1) separate (2) private property.

shrow : shrew.

sign : outward appearance.

slop : baggy breeches.

small : lower part of the leg.

smock : lady's nightdress.

sneaping : nipping.

sorel : buck of the fourth year.

sovereign : supreme.

specialties : contracts.

spleen : excess of laughter.

squier : footrule.

state : demeanour, dignity.

states : estates.

still : continuously.

suggested : prompted.

suggestions : temptations.

superscript : address on a letter.

swain : countryman, rustic.

tabor : small drum.

task'd : tried.

teen : sorrow.

tender : offer.

tharborough : thirdborough, constable.

thrasonical : boastful.

trencher : wooden plate.

trencher-knight : hanger-on.

triumviry : party of three.

Troyan : gay lad.

tumbler : acrobat.

turtle : turtle dove, lover.

uncasing : taking off the coat.

unsallied : unsullied.

ushering : escorting the ladies.

utter'd : put up for sale.

vailing : lowering.

varnish : outward gloss.

venue : bout (in fencing).

via : come on.

volable : quick.

vulgar : common tongue.

weeds : garments.

weigh : counterbalance.

welkin : sky.

well-liking : sleek.

wight : man.

wimpled : hooded.

wink : shut the eyes.

wort : sweet unfermented beer.

wot : know.

wreathed : folded.

ycliped : called.

zany : stooge.